Philosophy and Catholic Theology

A Primer

Philip A. Egan

M
G

A Michael Glazier Book

LITURGICAL PRESS
Collegeville, Minnesota

www.litpress.org

A Michael Glazier Book published by Liturgical Press

Cover design by David Manahan, OSB.
Cover illustration © 2009 Jupiterimages Corporation.

Library of Congress Cataloging-in-Publication Data

Egan, Philip A.
    Philosophy and Catholic theology : a primer / Philip A. Egan.
      p.   cm.
    Includes bibliographical references.
    ISBN 978-0-8146-5661-7 (pbk.)
      1. Catholic Church and philosophy.   2. Theology.   3. Catholic Church—Doctrines.   4. Philosophy and religion.   I. Title.
  BX1795.P47E24 2009
  230'.042—dc22
                    2008040187

Contents

Figures

Preface

This short primer was originally composed in a different and abbreviated format for the Maryvale Institute, Birmingham, and its excellent distance-learning BPhil degree in philosophy. It sought to address the needs of honors-level undergraduates studying philosophy, in order to outline some of the ways philosophy has influenced theology and in the process to offer those students a kind of *vademecum* of recent Catholic theology. This is why a basic knowledge of philosophy is presumed. The book has since been rewritten in its present form to be of interest to seminarians completing their studies of philosophy and beginning theology, particularly those studying foundational or fundamental theology. It has a revised aim of helping such students to navigate some of the current developments and trends in Catholic theology. However, I hope that, in addition to philosophy undergraduates and seminarians, this short work may be of interest to any student of theology and, indeed, to the general reader who is sensitive to or curious about the influence of philosophy on theology.

The intention throughout has been to avoid excessive technical detail or coverage of matters of academic dispute, except those necessary to our purpose. The book prefers to offer a straightforward survey or overview. Such a project by its nature has to be highly selective and cannot claim to be comprehensive. It reflects the views and interests of its author, who, in advance, apologizes to the reader for the omission of many names of philosophers and theologians and many developments and trends the reader might have wished to have seen included.

If the purpose of this primer is to map out the influence of contemporary philosophies on recent Catholic theology, then the task must necessarily be approached in stages. Thus chapter 1, "Theology," begins with a discussion of what theology is about and how much human reason—and therefore philosophy—has a role in it and what the nature of that role might be. The Catholic tradition has taken a keen and nuanced view of these matters, and so, following the mainstream of that tradition, we look at the role of reason in the theological process, the history of theology, the questions theology deals with, its foundations, and some of its basic parameters. Extensive use is made in this section of magisterial statements that have established a clear direction for subsequent theology, namely, the Dogmatic Constitution on the Catholic Faith (*Dei Filius*) of the First Vatican Council (1870) and the Dogmatic Constitution on Divine Revelation (*Dei Verbum*) of the Second Vatican Council (1965). The relevant sections from the text of the former can be found in the appendix, and the relevant paragraphs from the latter were neatly summarized in the *Catechism of the Catholic Church* (80–95). As these magisterial pronouncements are explored, the chief counter positions are also discussed.

Chapter 2, "Recent Theology," is about the context in which theology has been done in the recent past and is being done today. The trends and developments that have taken place over the last hundred years or so are examined. Central to Catholic theology during this period has been the far-reaching process of change and renewal that led to Vatican II (1962–1965), and that in some respects caught the wider church unaware. We also discuss the progress made in the period since. The council had a profound and pervasive impact on every aspect of ecclesial life, and this section discusses the principal theological developments that have occurred, together with the key protagonists.

Chapter 3, "Philosophy and Theology," reaches the heart of the matter by exploring the influence of the various families of contemporary philosophy on this or that strand of theology, on this or that theologian, and on this or that theological issue. Such an enterprise has its risks, as the reader will appreciate, since it could easily fall prey to oversimplification, both philosophical and theological. This is why the author must state at the outset that he is not trying to sum up the history and concern of each philosophy mentioned or to suggest that any individual theologian is in the exclusive thrall of any particular philosophy, even though some theologians do acknowledge their dependence on particular philosophers or on rigorously grounded philosophical presuppositions. Rather, the aim of this section is simply to indicate general influences on a theologian's thought or work.

Chapter 4, "Theological Method," looks at some of the theological methods and features of theology from the past, at the functions of the creeds in the early period and the *quaestio disputata* in the Middle Ages, and then how the challenges of the Reformation and modernity were met by neoscholasticism and its thesis theology. After discussing the crisis of method following Vatican II, the second half of the section explores some of the current "styles" of theology and their philosophical underpinnings.

It would be impossible to offer a primer like this from a supposedly neutral perspective, and in any case this is not our purpose. The concept of theology here is avowedly Roman Catholic, or at least its intention is to fit squarely within the mainstream of the Roman Catholic tradition, giving due value to the statements of the Roman magisterium relating to theology, faith, and reason. I hope, too, that this work will recall aspects of these issues that other Roman Catholic theologians may have neglected. Yet it does all of this irenically and with a critical awareness of the challenges put to the tradition. In any case, much of what is said is not exclusive to the Roman Catholic tradition, and I hope that readers from the Orthodox, Protestant, and Reformed traditions will find in the text useful paradigms and examples to illuminate their own thinking. Where practicable, cross-references to theologians and trends within Orthodox, Protestant, and Reformed theology are incorporated.

Finally, the reader will also notice the influence on this text of the Thomist tradition in general and of the Canadian Jesuit philosopher and theologian Bernard Lonergan (1904–84) in particular.

I give thanks to Our Lord Jesus Christ, who has given me the great privilege of sharing in his sacred priesthood. I would also like to thank the Most Rev. Brian Noble, bishop of Shrewsbury, for his trust, prayers, and untiring support; Father Joseph Flanagan and the Lonergan Institute at Boston College for their encouragement and the wherewithal that enabled the writing of this book; Father Mark Crisp and the staff of St. Mary's College Oscott for their friendship and Christian example; the students of the college for patiently sitting through my lectures; and Dr. Andrew Beards and those at the Maryvale Institute, Birmingham, for inviting me to make a contribution to their philosophy program.

Philip Egan
St. Mary's College Oscott
26 January 2008

Chapter One

Theology

In the Western tradition, philosophy (Greek *philos*, "friend," and *sophia*, "wisdom") is generally understood to encompass the study and discussion of the correct principles of reasoning (logic), the manner by which human knowing takes place (epistemology), the nature of reality and what exists (metaphysics), and how we should live (ethics). Philosophy, as distinct from theology, claims to base itself solely on rational arguments that prescind from any act of, or commitment to religious faith and belief, although there are branches of philosophy that discuss faith and religion, such as philosophy of religion. Philosophy, then, is a product of human reason. But to understand the influence of contemporary philosophies on recent Catholic theology we must also discuss what we mean by theology, because in some conceptions of theology, human reason is deemed to have little or no formal part. If this is the case, then we cannot raise the question of how contemporary philosophies influence theology. So the first question is: What is theology? What is it about? What is theology for and what does it seek to do? This chapter discusses the nature and functions of theology, and the relationship of reason to theology. Our answers to these questions—about the relationship between faith and reason, and the theology to which it gives birth—will pave the way for a study of the influence of philosophy on theology.

1. *Dei Filius* and the Interrelationship of Faith and Reason

The term theology, first used by Origen (d. 254), comes from the Greek *theou logos*, literally discourse or reasoning about God. Theology can be understood to be the rational study of God and religious belief, and in a specifically Christian understanding it is the rational study of the revelation God has given in Jesus Christ. In other words, let us establish the following statement as a working definition to guide our reflections in this first section:

> Christian theology is the systematic study of God's self-revelation in Jesus Christ. It also studies the human experience, understanding, knowledge, and reception of this revelation, and in particular how Christian disciples are expected to live their lives.

This working definition is not meant to be either exhaustive or novel. Indeed, it concurs more or less with the medieval understanding. To medievals the first object of theology was God's own self, God *qua* God, or as St. Thomas Aquinas (d. 1274) put it, *Deus sub ratione Dei* (*Summa Theologiae* [henceforth ST] I-I, q. 1, a. 7), and everything that follows from that, namely, creation in its relationship to God. Contemporary theologies, however, have considerably developed and expanded the way the scope and purpose of theology can be understood. Theologians in the modern era have adopted biblical and historical approaches to theology that focus on the person and work of Christ, his life, death, and resurrection, and how in him the God of salvation has saved and liberated human beings. Again, many recent theologians have espoused an "anthropological turn" in one form or other. They try to see things from an earthly, human perspective, investigating the relevance of divine revelation for humanity and its transforming effect upon the various domains of secular life. They take seriously the belief that the Son of God became incarnate, died, and rose again *pro nobis*, that is, for us and for our salvation.

The working definition envisages theology as based on divine revelation. This has important implications. Is theology the product of divine revelation alone: "This is what God has revealed"? Or does it involve human reasoning: "This is what we understand God's revelation means for us"? Is theology, as some fundamentalist Christians believe, a body of knowledge that has been passed down in the Bible and/or through the church that must be unthinkingly received, believed, and put into practice? Or is it, as some liberal Christians believe, a kind of philosophical reflection on revelation such that anyone, believer or not, can undertake it? Further, is faith necessary—do you need to be a practicing Christian—to do Christian theology? The First Vatican Council (1869–70) dealt authoritatively with many of these questions in its Dogmatic Constitution on the Catholic Faith, *Dei Filius*. The important yet highly nuanced statement about the relationship of faith and reason that Vatican I made was largely reiterated by John Paul II in his 1998 encyclical *Fides et Ratio*.

Faith or Reason? Or Faith and Reason?

The relationship between faith and reason was much debated in the nineteenth century chiefly because of the new and challenging philosophies then current, originating in the Enlightenment, together with the rush of new scientific discoveries and technological advances. All of these seemed to underline the power of human reason to reorder nature with confidence and to construct a new, human-made world. In theology the new ideas raised questions about the extent and limits of human reason in relation to the Christian faith. The ongoing controversies over the teaching of Louis Bautain (d. 1867), professor of philosophy at Strasbourg; Cardinal Louis-Jacques-Maurice de Bonald (d. 1870); Felicité de Lamennais (d. 1854), who later formally renounced his Catholic beliefs; Augustin Bonnetty (d. 1879), a major proponent of traditionalism; and Georg Hermes (d. 1831), the controversial professor of dogmatic theology at Bonn, provoked numerous interventions from the Vatican as well as two encyclical letters from Pius IX warning of the dangers: *Qui Pluribus* (1846) and *Quanta Cura* (1864). Attached to the latter was the celebrated *Syllabus of Condemned Errors*.

It is worth noting here some of the early propositions of the *Syllabus* dealing with absolute rationalism and moderate rationalism, both of which were condemned:

> 4. All religious truths originate from the natural power of human reason. Hence reason is the principal norm by which we can and must reach knowledge of whatever kind of truths.

> . . .

> 6. Faith in Christ is detrimental to human reason and divine revelation not only is of no use but is even harmful to human perfection.

> . . .

> 8. Since human reason is on a par with religion itself, theological disciplines have to be handled in the same manner as the philosophical ones.

> . . .

> 9. All dogmas of the Christian religion are, without distinction, the object of natural science or of philosophy; human reason solely as developed in history can, by means of its natural powers and principles, come to a true understanding of all, even the more profound dogmas, provided only that such dogmas be proposed to reason as its object.

> . . .

11. The church must not only abstain from any censure of philosophy; she must also tolerate the errors of philosophy, and leave it to philosophy to correct itself.

. . .

14. Philosophy is to be treated without taking any account of supernatural revelation. (Pius IX, *Syllabus of Condemned Errors*, DS 2904, 2906, 2908-9, 2911, and 2914/ ND 112)

These disputes about faith and reason formed the background to *Dei Filius* (1870). It is interesting, in this context, to compare and contrast the philosophical context of Vatican I with that of Pope John Paul II's encyclical letter *Fides et Ratio* (1998). Whereas in the nineteenth century the critical issue was faith, and whether faith could convey knowledge additional to that attained by human reason, for John Paul II the various postmodern philosophies of deconstruction had undermined human reason and made reason the critical issue, particularly whether human reason could know anything at all with certainty. In fact, it could be argued, the relationship of faith and reason continues to be highly controversial in the early twenty-first century. The philosophico-theological discussion of how faith and reason might be correlated distinguishes Christianity from the other major religions. In his "Address to Scientists at the University of Regensburg" (2006), Pope Benedict XVI explored the use of reason in religion, making the provocative point that if creation had not been made through *Logos*, the Word, then God could presumably ask humans to perform nonreasonable deeds and actions that might even be extreme.

The issue of the relationship between faith and reason raises at least three clusters of questions. First, what is the nature of faith? Is it reasonable? Or is the Christian faith principally a feeling, as Friedrich Schleiermacher (d. 1834) asserted, or a leap in the dark, as Søren Kierkegaard (d. 1855) put it?

Second, does revelation reveal things that are not knowable by reason? Or are the Christian faith and its teachings perfectly reasonable, even rationally demonstrable? Immanuel Kant (d. 1804) spoke of a "religion within the bounds of pure reason." In other words, would it be true to say that what Christians believe about love—that people should refrain from murder, violence, injustice, and oppression—should make as much sense to an unbeliever as to a believer?

A third complex of questions arises around the precise nature of the relationship between faith and reason. For instance: how, if at all, does theology relate to other fields of knowledge? Does it in any way connect with the empirical sciences, natural and human? Indeed, could there ever be a contradiction between the principles, positions, and results of theology and those of the sciences, and if so, how might it be resolved and which discipline might have the priority?

Christians might respond to these issues in one of two ways. On the one hand, evangelicals, following the direction set by Martin Luther (d. 1546) and Karl Barth (d. 1968), insist on *sola fide*, faith alone. Faith is far more important than reason. Indeed, the only thing that matters is a personal faith in Jesus Christ. The original sin of Adam and Eve has left humanity a *massa damnata*, with nothing to be proud of. Even reason has been darkened. Before the sheer truth, reality, justice, and glory of God, revealed above all on the cross of Christ, the intellect is like a mirror that has been smashed, the glass emptied out. Humans can know little or nothing about God by the light of natural reason. Jesus Christ alone is the Way, the Truth, and the Light, and it is thanks to his revelation that the saving truths about God are known.

Other Christians have rejected this line of thinking and, largely under the influence of nineteenth-century rationalism and twentieth-century liberalism, have opted instead to subject faith and the teachings of Christianity to reason alone, and even to personal choice and opinion. In this view the human intellect has not been damaged at all by the Fall. Reason is a gift God has given to humans so that they can find the truth and discern the right way to live.

Vatican I took a middle line on these debates. The council envisaged faith and reason as complementary, that is, as mutually and intrinsically interrelated. Human reason was damaged by original sin but not destroyed. The mirror had been cracked, but it was still serviceable. According to *Dei Filius*, divine revelation not only helps humans to cope with those cracks, confirming things that reason can see, but in addition gives access to many other matters of faith that would not otherwise have been known. Thus, the council declared, there are some theological realities that can be known through ordinary human knowing. Some theologians list examples of these, such as the presence of the soul, the existence of God, the reality of human freedom, the natural law, the promise of immortality, and the hope of an afterlife. There are, in addition, many other truths revealed to humanity by Jesus Christ, and these are known by faith.

Vatican I, therefore, stressed two kinds of knowledge: what can be known through reason and what can be known through revelation, the two orders (reason and faith) being not opposed but mutually interrelated.

This position was reiterated by John Paul II in the opening sentence of the encyclical *Fides et Ratio*:

> Faith and reason are like two wings on which the human spirit rises to the contemplation of truth; and God has placed in the human heart a desire to know the truth—in a word, to know himself—so that, by knowing and loving God, men and women may also come to the fullness of truth about themselves. (John Paul II, *Fides et Ratio*, n. 1)

In other words, human knowledge (e.g., science, medicine, and critical scholarship) and religion have one and the same aim, to know the truth. This is why it is not perhaps an overstatement to assert that in the Catholic tradition a high value has always been given to philosophy, science, the arts, and scholarship.

The Dogmatic Constitution of Vatican I, Dei Filius

In *Qui Pluribus, Quanta Cura,* and the *Syllabus of Condemned Errors*, Pius IX condemned two opposing theological trends that were also addressed by Vatican I in *Dei Filius*. These were "fideism-traditionalism" and "rationalism-liberalism."

To begin with the first pairing: Fideism is the belief that God can only be known by faith and by what he has revealed to us in Jesus Christ. In other words, human reasoning, philosophy, and natural theology tell us nothing about God. Religious truth requires a "leap in the dark"; it might be recognizable by an instinct (Charles Sanders Peirce) or in our feelings (Friedrich Schleiermacher) but not by the intellect. Most Catholic theologians eschewed these views, which were being proposed by certain Protestant or Reformed theologies, notably those of an evangelical or fundamentalist kind, but some of them espoused traditionalism, a kind of Catholic version of fideism. Traditionalism was found in various ways in the nineteenth-century writers mentioned above, notably de Lamennais, Bonald, Bautain, and Bonnetty. Traditionalism asserted that unaided natural reason could not come to know God independently from belonging to or being brought up within a religious tradition, such as being a member of the church. Taken together, therefore, fideism-traditionalism was a distrust of reason, suggesting that faith is ultimately not something rational but what "we just have to accept."

Rationalism-liberalism, on the other hand, took the opposite line. Rationalism and liberalism made human reason the only or the chief resource and faculty of humans. Rationalism, in other words, subjects divine revelation to the judgment of human reason: This or that should be believed because it is rationally coherent or reasonably demonstrable. The tenets of rationalism can be seen in the project of the philosopher Immanuel Kant, whose thought has permeated the modern era. Rationalism can also be discerned before Kant in the writings of François-Marie Voltaire (d. 1778), a lifelong enemy of Catholicism and the vigorous opponent of Blaise Pascal.

Another version of rationalism can be found in the thought of Georg Hermes, whose propositions Pius IX condemned in *Qui Pluribus*. Hermes, whose lifelong ambition was to meet the challenge of Kant, wanted to demonstrate the harmony between faith and reason, giving thereby a secure ground or basis to the truth claims of faith. For example, in his *Positive Einleitung* (1829) he tackled five questions: Are the books of the New Testament externally (historically) true? Is the oral tradition involved in the New Testament historically true? Are the expositions and interpretations of the teaching of Jesus as presented by the church infallibly correct? Is the teaching of Jesus as contained in the New Testament intrinsically true? And are the teachings of Jesus handed down by tradition intrinsically true? Hermes argued that knowledge is subjectively true when we become convinced in our minds that it coincides with its object. But he departed from the Catholic tradition in asserting that the grounds for assent were the same in matters of faith as in every other area of human knowing: what compels is an argument's inner logic ("Hermesianism"). Hermesianism was condemned by the Roman magisterium because it was perceived to be a brand of rationalism. It allegedly reduced divine revelation to human knowing, bringing the truths of faith revealed on the authority of Christ before the bar of human reason while suppressing the supernatural element.

Liberalism in religious and theological matters is somewhat more complex. It eludes an easy definition, partly because it has meant different things at different times. However, for simplicity here we may say that in nineteenth-century terms it was the next step beyond rationalism. Liberalism arguably reduced religion, revelation, and the truths of faith to personal opinion or individual taste, and thus paved the way for early twentieth-century modernism (see below). John Henry Newman (d. 1890) declared himself an opponent of liberalism. He saw himself as engaged in a lifelong battle against it, once famously describing it in his *An Essay on the Development of Christian Doctrine* (1845) as "the anti-dogmatic principle":

> That truth and falsehood in religion are but matter of opinion; that one doctrine is as good as another; that the Governor of the world does not intend that we should gain the truth; that there is no truth; that we are not more acceptable to God by believing this than by believing that; that no one is answerable for his opinions; that they are a matter of necessity or accident; that it is enough if we sincerely hold what we profess; that our merit lies in seeking, not in possessing; that it is a duty to follow what seems to us true, without a fear lest it should not be true; that it may be a gain to succeed, and can be no harm to fail; that we may take up and lay down opinions at pleasure; that belief belongs to the mere intellect, not to the heart also; that we may safely trust to ourselves in matters of Faith, and need no other guide—this is the principle of philosophies and heresies, which is very weakness. (John Henry Newman, *An Essay on the Development of Christian Doctrine*, 357–58)

The various shades and positions involved in fideism-traditionalism and rationalism-liberalism are complex. Basically, *Dei Filius* traced a middle line between the extremes. It asserted that faith and reason were mutually and intrinsically interrelated. Unaided reason could give us some (certain) knowledge about God and the basic truths of faith, but the gift of faith in divine revelation enabled us to know and be certain about many other truths that would not be knowable by reason alone.

Since Vatican I drew on common elements from the scholastic tradition and in *Dei Filius* established parameters within which most Roman Catholic theologians have operated ever since, it is worth delaying a moment to examine the detail of the council's statements. The relevant sections of the text can be found in the appendix. Here we note four points.

First, on the natural knowledge of God, God can be known by reason alone:

> [The church] holds and teaches that God, the source and end of all things, can be known with certainty from the things that were created, through the natural light of human reason . . . [and] that truths about things divine which of themselves are not beyond human reason can, even in the present condition of humankind, be known by everyone with facility, with firm certitude and with no admixture of error. (Vatican I *Dei Filius*, DS 3004-5/ND 113-44)

Dei Filius asserted that humans can know that God exists, and that they can know certain things about God by the light of unaided human reason. In other words, belief in God can be proved (in the sense of demonstrated or shown) to be reasonable, to be a rationally and logically coherent stance. Moreover, as noted above, certain basic truths of faith can be known: that God is personal, that humans have souls and that the soul is immortal, that there is a natural law implanted in human conscience, and that heaven is the final goal. These truths of faith can be known by reason alone, according to *Dei Filius*. Moreover, these are truths of faith that have been confirmed by the revelation given in Jesus Christ, and so they can also be known—and indeed, much more can be said about them—through faith. (See figure 1.) Revelation and the gift of faith may be said to enable this basic knowledge to be transcended, and so humans can enter into a real, intimate, and personal relationship with God.

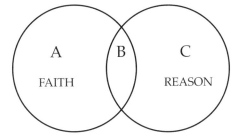

THE USE OF HUMAN REASON ACCORDING TO *DEI FILIUS*

A — FAITH B C — REASON

In other words, the secular and sacred arenas can overlap. Thus, we know some things as revealed by faith (A), some through reason (C), and some—recalling what was said above about natural knowledge of God—are accessible to both (B). Simple examples might be: (A) the doctrine of the Blessed Trinity, (C) the structure of DNA, and (B) the existence of God.

Figure 1

It is worth adding a couple of notes here. In an essay called "Natural Knowledge of God" in *A Second Collection*, Bernard Lonergan made the important observation that while *Dei Filius* said that theoretically it was possible to know God and certain basic truths about God and our salvation, it did not say that this was the manner by which people actually did come to know God. It said only that it was possible. In practice, Lonergan said, most people—especially today—would need the help of grace and the gift of faith to overcome the cultural factors and intellectual baggage that often obscure this knowledge. Moreover, on another point, we might note how the *Catechism of the Catholic Church* (CCC) 31-35 handles and develops the teaching of *Dei Filius*. When it speaks about knowing for certain about the existence of God, it says that the knowledge of God's existence is not like a proof from the empirical sciences, but rather a collection of "converging and convincing arguments" based on the world humans know and on the marvel of the human person.

Our second point to note is that divine revelation and human reason yield two orders of knowledge:

> There is a twofold order of knowledge, distinct not only in its source but also in its object; in its source, because in the one we know by natural reason, in the other by divine faith; in its object, because apart from what natural reason can attain, there are proposed to our belief mysteries that are hidden in God, which can never be known unless they are revealed by God. (*Dei Filius*, DS 3015/ND 131)

In other words, here *Dei Filius* states that there are two orders of knowledge: that which comes through reason and that which comes through revelation. They differ in their source—one is from human observation, the other from God—and in their object: one is the realm of things known by human reason, the other the realm of things revealed by God. According to the council, therefore, human knowing can take two forms: religious knowing (knowing illuminated by faith) and nonreligious knowing (all other forms of knowing or "reason"). What differentiates them is the object known (either revealed or known by human observation) and the knowing subject (the human being using faith-filled reason or the human being using ordinary reason). If a person has faith and is in love with God, he or she, when exploring the objects of revelation, can discern things not visible to a nonreligious knower. A nonreligious knower might theoretically know about God's existence, the immortality of the soul, and, say, the natural law but not about the Trinity, the divinity of Christ, or the sacraments.

The third point is that Vatican I states that faith is a divine gift enabling reason to perceive, understand, come to know, and put into practice the mysteries it cannot exhaust:

> If reason illumined by faith inquires in an earnest, pious and sober manner, it attains by God's grace a certain understanding of the mysteries, which is most fruitful, both from the analogy with the objects of its natural knowledge and from the connection of these mysteries with one another and with our ultimate end. But it never

becomes capable of understanding them in the way it does the truths which constitute its proper object. (*Dei Filius*, DS 3016/ND 132)

Reason, according to *Dei Filius*, has an important role in matters of faith. It has the task, when graced by faith, of perceiving revealed truths and of penetrating, exploring, interpreting, asserting, and putting them into practice. On the other hand, human knowing is also limited, and so humans can only come to a certain understanding of the divine mysteries. Subsequently the 1992 *Catechism of the Catholic Church* 39-43 reprised and expanded the teaching of *Dei Filius*, saying that reason cannot "contain" God, but it can "attain" to God:

> 39. In defending the ability of human reason to know God, the Church is expressing her confidence in the possibility of speaking about him to all men and with all men, and therefore of dialogue with other religions, with philosophy and science, as well as with unbelievers and atheists.
> 40. Since our knowledge of God is limited, our language about him is equally so. We can name God only by taking creatures as our starting point, and in accordance with our limited human ways of knowing and thinking.
> . . .
> 42. God transcends all creatures. We must therefore continually purify our language of everything in it that is limited, image-bound or imperfect, if we are not to confuse our image of God—"the inexpressible, the incomprehensible, the invisible, the ungraspable" [Liturgy of *St. John Chrysostom*, Anaphora]—with our human representations. Our human words always fall short of the mystery of God.
> 43. Admittedly, in speaking about God like this, our language is using human modes of expression; nevertheless it really does attain to God himself, though unable to express him in his infinite simplicity. Likewise, we must recall that "between Creator and creature no similitude can be expressed without implying an even greater dissimilitude" [Lateran Council IV: DS 806]; and that "concerning God, we cannot grasp what he is, but only what he is not, and how other beings stand in relation to him." (CCC 39-40, 42-43)

Dei Filius mentions three "intellectual devices" human reasoning can use to expound the sacred mysteries: analogy, the *nexus mysteriorum inter se*, and the connection with our ultimate end. We will consider each of these in turn.

The first device mentioned is analogy, that is, reasoning by proportion or correspondence to realities that are similar to, and yet dissimilar from, those things known by unaided reason. Analogy has been the subject of much philosophical and theological discussion. Because Christ, "the Word through whom all things were made," used the whole created order as a means of communicating himself, he was able to use human words, images, and concepts to express the Word of God. This use of analogy is sometimes called the "principle of the incarnation." One example theologians sometimes give is how Christ saw in human paternity an image of his relationship with the Father. Other theologians have used other analogies and in a more speculative manner. For instance, Augustine's (d. 430) theology of the Trinity depends on his use of the analogy of the powers of the soul: the intellect, the memory, and the will.

The second device mentioned is the *nexus mysteriorum inter se* ("the interconnection of mysteries among themselves"). Scholastic theology believed that all the mysteries of faith were interconnected and that the revealed truth as a totality formed an organic whole, simple and utterly coherent, with no self-contradictory elements. Scholastic thinkers reasoned that because each particular aspect or expression of faith would fit in with every other aspect, it is possible in some theological reflections to proceed by argument from examples in one area of theology to conclusions in another, discovering the multiple ways the truths of faith are interlinked within an overall harmony. *Dei Filius* seems to support this idea that individual mysteries of faith evoke and answer each other. For example, what the gospels record about the risen body of Christ after his resurrection can enable theologians to reach tentative conclusions about eschatology and about the condition of all humans after the resurrection of the body.

Finally, *Dei Filius* refers to the use of the "connection of the mysteries with our ultimate end," that is, the relation of the present reality to its eschatological goal. This is the argument that what is dim and unclear now will be made bright and clear then. What is suggested, imperfect, or incomplete in this world will in the next be made perfect, complete, and fulfilled. In this manner, Vatican I asserted, theological reasoning is able in some cases to extrapolate from what is known now to what might be the case in the future.

According to *Dei Filius*, then, reason illumined by faith can reach a certain limited understanding of the mysteries. Eastern Orthodox theologies tend, in contrast to Western theologies, to be much more "apophatic" (Greek *apo*, "other than," and *phaio*, "to bring to light"). They often hesitate before forming concepts of God and are negatively self-expressive, saying what God is not. The *Catechism of the Catholic Church* 39-43 seems to be more congruent with such Eastern accents. Western theologies, on the other hand, tend to be more "kataphatic" (Greek *kata*, "down from above"). They underline the incarnation, how the eternal entered time, that the Word became flesh, and that Christ spoke the Word of God in human words (Vatican II, *Dei Verbum* 4). *Dei Filius*, while acknowledging the limits, could be said to be firmly in that Western tradition when it goes on to assert that theology can truly say something. To speak of God revealing mysteries, according to Vatican I, is not to imply that there is nothing that can be said or that these are things that cannot at all be understood. A mystery here signifies a "sacred reality." These sacred realities are ineffable and inexhaustible, so great that although something can be said, their intelligibility can never be exhausted. They can be revisited time and again, and they will always manifest something new. Perhaps a good analogy for this is the notion of love. To conceptualize love or to attempt to contain in a definition what is meant by love is always elusive. Indeed, it is impossible, which is why authors can write books and books about love until the end of time. This is arguably even more the case when speaking of the theological notion of love, *caritas*, since God is love. God has revealed his love in the gift of himself, Jesus Christ. Love is a Person, and so love is much greater, deeper, and richer than any propositional truth or rational conclusion to an argument.

The council's statements bring to mind a further illustration, the famous story of Augustine meeting a boy on the beach. The boy had dug a hole in the sand and was running to and from the sea with buckets of water. When Augustine asked him what he was doing, he said he was trying to empty the sea into the hole. "But that's impossible!" Augustine said. "I know," the boy replied, "but I'll be able to do that before you can 'get into your head' the mystery of the Trinity." Or again, all the books in the world cannot exhaust the meaning of the parables in the gospels—but that does not stop exegetes from writing about them or preachers from giving homilies.

A fourth and final point from *Dei Filius* is its statement that faith and reason are mutually supportive, although the truths of faith have priority (DS 3017-19). These later paragraphs have provided Catholic theology with some important principles. In the conception of the council, although faith is above reason, faith and reason are interrelated and so cannot contradict each other. There cannot be double truths:

> [Although] faith is above reason, there can never be a real conflict
> between faith and reason, since the same God who reveals mysteries
> and infuses faith has bestowed the light of reason on the human

mind, and God cannot deny himself, nor can truth ever contradict truth. (*Dei Filius*, DS 3017/ND 133)

The argument is from Aquinas: it is the same God who grounds all truth, whether secular or divine, and the truth is ultimately one. Where a contradiction becomes apparent this is because, *Dei Filius* claims, either dogmas have not been interpreted properly or understood authentically, or a flawed scientific or critical theory is being proposed as certain:

> The deceptive appearance of . . . a contradiction is mainly due to the fact that either the dogmas of faith have not been understood and expounded according to the mind of the church, or that uncertain theories are taken for verdicts of reason. (*Dei Filius*, DS 3017/ND 133)

However, faith and reason can work to assist each other:

> Not only can there be no conflict between faith and reason, but they also support each other, since right reason demonstrates the foundations of faith and, illumined by its light, pursues the understanding of divine things, while faith frees and protects reason from errors and provides it with manifold insights. (*Dei Filius*, DS 3019/ND 135)

This is why, the dogmatic constitution adds, the church promotes all the sound activities of human reason such as science, medicine, the arts, culture, and scholarship:

> It is therefore far removed from the truth to say that the Church opposes the study of human arts and sciences; on the contrary, she supports and promotes them in many ways. She does not ignore or despise the benefits that human life derives from them. Indeed, she confesses that as they have their origin from God who is the Lord of knowledge (cf. 1 Samuel 2:3), so too, if rightly pursued, they lead to God with the help of his grace. (*Dei Filius*, DS 3019/ND 135)

This point was subsequently taken up by Vatican II in *Gaudium et Spes*: the church upholds the legitimate autonomy of the sciences, and of human affairs and organizations, together with their methods, while insisting only that such disciplines not impinge on matters of faith:

> Nor does the Church in any way forbid that these sciences, each in its sphere, should make use of their own principles and of the method proper to them. While, however, acknowledging this just

freedom, she seriously warns lest they fall into error by going contrary to divine doctrine, or, stepping beyond their own limits, they enter into the sphere of faith and create confusion. (*Gaudium et Spes* 36)

Nonetheless, according to Vatican I, the contents of revelation have a priority because they have been revealed by Christ. The church has the task of propounding them in every age and place, and it cannot err. Christians, therefore, must not hold scientific or scholarly positions that are inimical to faith:

> Believing Christians are not only forbidden to defend as legitimate conclusions of science such opinions which they realize to be contrary to the doctrine of faith, particularly if they have been condemned by the church, but they are seriously bound to account them as errors which put on the fallacious appearance of truth. (*Dei Filius*, DS 3018/ ND 134)

Chapter 4 of the Constitution concludes with canons condemning rationalism (DS 3041), those who propose the absolute autonomy of the human sciences (DS 3042), and the future tenet of the modernists, that advances in science can revise the truths of revelation (DS 3043).

To sum up: *Dei Filius* is said to have traced a middle line between the extremes of fideism-traditionalism and rationalism-liberalism. It asserted that faith and reason were mutually and intrinsically interrelated, that unaided reason could yield some (certain) knowledge about God, but that the gift of faith enables humans to know much more. Faith is not subject to reason (rationalism), or reason to blind faith (fideism). Moreover, faith and reason should not be seen dualistically, as some have done since then, as totally discrete realms in which the sacred and the secular, theology and philosophy, religion and science are divorced, with nothing to say to each other. Rather, one human reasoning process is operative in science, scholarship, and practical affairs, but when enlightened by faith, graced reason can perceive, understand, know, and put into practice the saving knowledge that God has revealed in Christ.

In all these subtle and complex position statements on faith and reason, and on the use of reason within theology, Vatican I established certain general parameters within which Catholic thinkers in the main have operated since. However, the nineteenth-century issue was not only about the use of reason within theology but also about the nature of faith. So now we must ask: What is faith? This also brings us back to one of the original questions: Is faith necessary for the study of theology? Or is theology simply a work of reason, a critical reflection on revelation such that anyone, believer or not, could do it?

Faith, Reason, and Theology

Our working definition of theology envisaged theology as a reasoned reflection on divine revelation. We then critically examined the meaning of this in relation to the principles regarding faith and reason articulated by Vatican Council I in *Dei Filius*. Theology is faith-filled reason attempting better to understand its object—God—and humanity in relation to God. It involves a constant exchange between faith and reason, the sacred and the secular, religion and culture. It is a reasoned reflection on the Word of God that attempts to grasp the significance of that Word for oneself and for humanity. It follows that theology in the sense outlined here requires the theologian to be a man or woman with faith. Even if, as we shall see, there are aspects or tasks in the overall theological enterprise for which a personal faith commitment is of lesser importance, in general, if the conception of theology discussed so far is accepted, faith is required in order to do theology. This needs to be unpacked.

What is faith? Neoscholastic theology usefully distinguished the *fides quae creditur* ("the faith that is believed"), that is, the content and truths of faith revealed by God, "The Faith," from the *fides qua creditur* ("the faith by which is believed"), that is, the action of the human subject receiving the gift of faith, one's freely given faith response and adherence, under the influence of grace, to God's salvific offer, the act of believing the Word of God and committing oneself to it.

An act of faith (*fides qua*) could be said to be the complete homage and submission of mind and will to God, assenting to what God has revealed (*fides quae*). This act is made because of who God is: God. It is a quality and virtue that flows from love, a gift of the Holy Spirit who floods the heart, enabling the believer to perceive, understand, and know things others cannot. In the phrase of the famous French religious philosopher and Christian apologist Blaise Pascal (d. 1662), "the heart has reasons that reason does not have." Bernard Lonergan captured the meaning of this well in his splendid saying: "Faith is the knowledge born of religious love" (*Method in Theology*, 115).

For the Christian, the faith response to God needs to incorporate a faith response to God's self-manifestation in Jesus Christ, and then, in the Catholic understanding, this faith response must also include, in a derivative manner, faith in the church, established by Christ to preserve and articulate his teaching. The *Catechism of the Catholic Church* explains this by noting that faith is not an isolated act. The Catholic Christian is first and foremost a member of the church (CCC 166-69). This is because, it says, the church is the primordial believer bearing, nourishing, and sustaining the faith of the individual, the one through, with, and in Christ, and animated by the Holy Spirit, who, on behalf of humanity, responds to the Father, saying "I believe." Therefore the *credo* of an individual Christian—the *credo* of the individual theologian—always participates in the universal church's *credo* or act of faith. So, summing all this up, we could say that for the theologian to do theology in the sense being envisaged here, she or he must have a faith commitment that is threefold: divine (faith in God), Christian (faith in Jesus Christ), and ecclesial (faith in the church as the divinely authorized guarantor of faith).

Dei Filius envisaged God bestowing a double gift: revelation in Christ (*fides quae*) and the faith needed for the human subject to accept it and adhere to it (*fides qua*). Faith, then, according to Vatican I, is a gift freely given by God that humans are always free to accept or reject. It is ever true: "you can lead a horse to water, but you cannot make it drink." The gift of faith—theological, christological, and ecclesial—gives rise to theology, faith enabling believers to perceive, penetrate, know, accept, and put into practice the revelation God has given. Faith enables believers to have certainty about the truths God has revealed, and faith helps them penetrate the sacred mysteries, although always with a limited understanding. Faith as God's continuing gift helps theologians to advance in understanding, to grow in knowledge, and to conform themselves ever more perfectly to what God is revealing. This is not to say that faith is blind. As *Dei Filius* suggested by speaking of a relationship between faith and reason, faith needs to be critical since it involves the use of reason with all its capacities, procedures, and hesitancy. Reason makes use of all its usual exigencies, thus enabling theology to engage in a constant critical exchange as the theologian reflects on God's revelation and its meaning.

If, in the concept of theology as envisaged here, faith is required for doing theology, it could still be argued that some of the tasks theologians perform require a less explicit faith or personal commitment. They could be done by anyone with the requisite academic credentials. For instance, faith is not so much a requirement for textual research, work on the sacred languages, archaeology, and church history as for the tasks of fundamental theology, Christology, ecclesiology, liturgy, and pastoral theology. In some disciplines of theology having faith might be a great help in motivating one's research, yet many of the expected tasks could be carried out regardless of the theologian's own personal faith commitment. However, there are clearly other disciplines, such as liturgical, moral, and pastoral theology, where one could show that it is precisely the creative application of the theologian's faith commitment that determines the expectations, directs the project, and shapes the outcomes.

Can faith be "proved"? Can theology prove that the mysteries of faith are true? Theology, in the sense discussed here, has its limits, because faith, as *Dei Filius* argued, is a divine gift. Reason, therefore, could not implant faith or gain it as the conclusion to an argument. Rather, reason "stands underneath" faith and submits to it. Consequently, theology would be unable to prove the truth of faith by operating in the same inductive manner as the empirical sciences, by an appeal to data. On the other hand, it could be argued that it is the task of theology, particularly those branches of theology connected with apologetics, to demonstrate the mysteries of faith or even faith itself to be reason-able. To believe could be shown to be the most attentive, intelligent, reasonable, practical, and charitable response to the mystery and gift of human existence.

2. Theology as an Academic Discipline

In this section we will develop some further implications of our definition of theology: After all, if theology requires faith on the part of the theologian, in what sense can we call it an academic or critical discipline?

It could be argued that every Christian does theology insofar as he or she reflects on the experience of faith or tries to understand its teaching and how to put that teaching into practice in his or her life. The history of theology is in effect the history of Christian reflection on the church's experience of faith. Even as an academic discipline at its most technical or most esoteric, theology is still a prolongation of that basic Christian reflection on lived experience. What differentiates academic theology from simple reflection on experience is its style; it proceeds in an academically self-conscious manner. It develops principles, critically examines its sources, follows appropriate methods, and devises serviceable procedures and applications.

Theology became a formally academic discipline in the Middle Ages, when it also began to become more diversified and specialized. Thus Aquinas differentiated theology as the study of revealed truth from what he called "natural theology." Natural theology specialized in what could be known about God through the use of the natural light of human reason but without revelation, that is, through critical reflection on the universe, the created order, human history, and the course of events. In the fourteenth and fifteenth centuries, spirituality, philosophy, and canon law also became distinct fields or areas of theology. In the eighteenth century modern historical-critical methods of scriptural exegesis turned biblical studies into a clearly discrete department of theology; subsequently the specialization of church history has also become a separate discipline. Today theology incorporates a large number of particular studies, divided either into disciplines such as dogma, biblical studies, spirituality, morals, liturgy, pastoral theology, patristics, and so on, or into treatises such as Christology, ecclesiology, revelation, Trinity, creation, grace, the virtues, and the sacraments. It often adopts historical (sometimes called "positive") and systematic (sometimes called "speculative" or hermeneutical) approaches.

How, then, might theology as an academic discipline be related to religion proper, the realm of revelation and faith? And on the other hand, how might theology be related to other related forms of critical scholarship such as religious studies?

Theology and Religion

Already in the early church a distinction had arisen between theology proper and religion proper. This is arguably evident in the writings of some of the Fathers of the church, that is, the great bishops, theologians, and writers of the first half of the first millennium. Most of these Fathers were not closeted academics but pastors, often with onerous and challenging responsibilities. Nonetheless, they produced some of the finest and most nuanced theological reflections of all time on the faith. Think of the sheer technical accomplishment of, for example, Augustine's *De Trinitate* (ca. 416) or the complex arguments of Athanasius (d. 373) in his *De Incarnatione Verbi Dei*. But the statements of the councils and synods of the fourth and fifth centuries began to reveal the development of a technical theology using philosophical terms and nonbiblical language to give a more precise articulation and definition of the tenets of Christian doctrine then in dispute. The classic example of this is the way the Council of Nicea (325) used the term *homoousios* (lit. "of the same substance") to pin down exactly the orthodox belief in the divinity of Christ. From that time onward theology began a long metamorphosis into an increasingly academic and "critical" discipline different from, although directed toward, religious faith. In effect, theology became a discourse one step removed from everyday religion and its observances. This process accelerated considerably in the medieval period. By the tenth and eleventh centuries the monastic schools adopted new, rigorous, and systematic methods for teaching theology. Attached to the great cathedrals, these schools eventually became Europe's first universities. In them theology was deemed to be the "queen of the sciences."

Today most theologians would agree that theology is not the same as religion. What Christians believe, what they practice, what they love is one thing (religion); how they express this, reflect on it, and critique it is another (theology). This is the background to the famous distinction Cardinal Newman drew in his autobiographical *Apologia pro Vita Sua* (1864) between a problem and a doubt: ten thousand difficulties do not make a doubt. In other words, theological problems are one thing, matters of faith and religion another. Religion is the lived reality of God's gift of divine love, the human response to the Gospel, whereas theology is the science or critical discipline that examines and discusses this. Some have described the difference as between the art of healing and the science of medicine. Theology may not be necessary for salvation, but Christians believe their religion is. Lonergan once compared the relationship between theology and religion to that between theory and reality, like the relationship of economics to running a business. A few theoretical difficulties about the economic indicators do not prevent the priest from receiving a Mass stipend! Yet religion does invite expression, and so religion and theology are intimately and mutually interconnected. They are to some extent in a dialectical relationship, theology being a theoretical withdrawal that intends a practical return.

Theology and Religious Studies

Many contemporary theologies are attempting to reaffirm their links with both spirituality, on the one hand, and daily life, on the other, restoring the holistic aspects of patristic theology. For Aquinas theology was both a science and a wisdom, that is, a body of organized knowledge about revelation and its meaning and also a practical and salvific philosophy of life (ST I-I, q. 1 a. 2 and a. 6). For him philosophy, theology, and spirituality were distinct yet held together. However, in the fourteenth century, as already mentioned, the study of logic and the exercise of human reasoning (philosophy) became distinct domains that would evolve along their own trajectories, somewhat independently from theology. Furthermore, with the rise of the *devotio moderna* at the same time, spirituality or ascetical theology began to be clearly differentiated from theology. Where theology dealt with intellectual and doctrinal knowledge about God, spirituality studied and gave advice about prayer, charity, mystical experience, and the disciple's personal relationship with God. The result of these developments and their subsequent evolution, many argued, left theology an increasingly intellectualist enterprise. Today many lament this and aspire to a reintegration of theology with spirituality. They reject tendencies that emphasize the intellectual dimension at the expense of the spiritual. Others, again against any tendency to intellectualism, insist on the Mystery of God that is theology's focus: what can be said about God and the mysteries of faith is nothing compared with what cannot be said. They recall how at the end of the *Summa Theologiae* Aquinas pronounced all his work "but straw" compared with the reality of meeting Christ.

Besides reforging the links with spirituality, other theologians express their concern with praxis: theology should not become so intellectualist or so mystical as to be divorced from practical matters and the pastoral application of the Gospel to daily life. This long-gestating concern with praxis reached a climax in the late twentieth century in the period after Vatican II. Karl Marx (d. 1883) had once argued that all religion was an opium, a drug that siphoned off the practical concern and lively energy of the working classes to better themselves and change their lot. Twentieth-century Christian apologetics took increasing note of this Marxist jibe, and in the immediate postconciliar period the Bavarian priest Johannes Baptist Metz (b. 1928) and other theologians associated with the journal *Concilium* endeavored to transcend the personalist categories and philosophies then in vogue in favor of a more practical social and political theology whose outcomes related to earthly concerns. Theology, they argued, should not be concerned merely with personal fulfillment, with ultimate issues, or with the spiritual context of life but should demonstrate how Christian discipleship is dynamically relevant to social, political, and economic issues, not least to the widespread poverty, suffering, and injustice many human beings undergo. This praxis critique has inspired many new theological trends in recent years, notably in liberation theologies, feminist thought, and environmental concern, as we shall see later.

In the working definition, faith is required for doing theology. This prerequisite of faith distinguishes theology from scientific studies of religion, usually called religious studies. The expansion of overseas travel and the discovery of hitherto unexplored ethnic cultures, together with the rise of critical historical scholarship from the eighteenth century onward, led to the emergence of new comparative studies of religion, religious belief systems, customs, practices, and traditions. Today religious studies explores beliefs, practices, and forms of religion in a comparative manner, with the aid of forms of scholarship that follow methods similar to those of the human sciences. It differs from theology in that it adopts a "from without" approach as opposed to a "from within" stance. Whereas theology is done from the perspective, or at least with the sympathy of, a committed believer, religious studies carefully avoids such religious truth-claims in favor of a phenomenological account of religion. It looks at the phenomena of religion, seeking to explore and categorize the common and distinctive features of the world's major religious traditions, their history and contemporary development. It employs historical, textual, philosophical, sociological, anthropological, and psychological methods. It explores cultural practices, anthropology, myth, and ritual. It discusses the big issues of life in a critical and informed manner, bringing together topics from ethics and philosophy, yet without any prior commitments of exclusivity. Indeed, at its best it seeks systematically to identify and categorize such commitments.

Finally, theology might be differentiated from "theological studies," that is, from the theology taught within Western and particularly British university theology departments. The principal distinction between theology and theological studies relates to christological and ecclesial foundation and context. The kind of theology conducted in a seminary, a religious house of formation, or a Catholic university differs from that done in the highly pluralistic theology faculties of a secular university. In the latter, while a theological context might generally be present— belief in God might be taken for granted, it being assumed that many of the lecturers and their students acknowledge a common faith in God—the christological and ecclesial contexts are often more ambiguous, pluralist, or secondary. Lecturers and students may have widely disparate religious and ecclesial commitments even though they might continue broadly to study this or that aspect of Christian (or other) theology. The courses offered—biblical studies, the history of doctrine, the study of religion, ethics, church history, etc.—reflect this situation. Often students in university theology departments are given a wide range of options to choose from: further study of the Bible or the Qurʾan, the philosophy of religion, religion within society and politics, contemporary spiritualities, religion within media and popular culture, and so on. The absence of common christological and ecclesial commitments, together with a wide-ranging syllabus of options, influences the style of theology, its purpose, and its methods. Courses in systematic theology tend to be few. Theology in a seminary is self-evidently geared toward the formation needed for pastoral ministry and religious life and so tends to aspire to a comprehensive overview, with few elective topics. Theological studies, however, are less narrowly focused, with the result that the curriculum is less comprehensive, less systematic, and less all-embracing, and more specialized, creative, and speculative. This creative form of theology, often done in conjunction with religious studies and frequently indistinguishable from it, leans toward hermeneutics, that is, theological commentaries on and insights into current problems or particular questions, typically the disputed issues of moral theology, authority in the church, or gender roles.

3. The History and Scope of Theology

Let us now turn to the history of theology and develop some further implications of our working definition of theology. The aim is not to offer a complete history or chronology of theology, but rather to discern in the evolution of theology what might be called its four principal "differentiations": thematic, doctrinal, systematic, and historical, reflecting the broadly different concerns theologians have had at different times in history.

In the early church the Fathers explored extensively the Divine Object of faith, that is, God himself, the person and nature of Christ, and the relations within the Blessed Trinity. These concerns were reflected in the great trinitarian and christological councils of the church in antiquity, which laid out in the creeds the principal tenets of orthodox doctrine. In the Middle Ages theologians focused more on matters of virtue and the moral life of the Christian. Many of the questions Aquinas tackles in the *Summa Theologiae* are about how to live a good life and reach the reward of heaven. Later, after the Protestant Reformation and the Council of Trent (1545–63), Catholic theology tended to concentrate on ecclesiology, that is, on the structure of the church and its authority, defending traditional doctrine from the critiques of the Reformers. It also gave attention during this period to the nature of the sacraments, as theologians developed many of the new medieval insights into liturgy and worship, such as the distinction between the natural and the supernatural or between matter and form. In the twentieth century, with its two world wars and the huge advances in science, medicine, and technology, pressing human issues have come to the fore. Consequently, it could be said that theology in the early twenty-first century is particularly concerned with anthropological issues and with the relevance of Christianity and religion in general to modernity: What is it to be human? What does the Christian faith say about modern living? How can Christian faith help build a better and more just world?

My thesis here is that behind the attention theology has given to all these different topics at different periods of history lie four fundamental "cognitional" questions that have structured and driven its concerns. These cognitional questions have to do with the sort of knowledge theology is considered to be. Is theology an account of experience? Does it yield the truth? What is its meaning? How has it varied over time and history? Each of these four questions emerged chronologically from the previous one while continuing to structure theological endeavors. Each in turn has led to what might be called a new differentiation within the theological enterprise.

In other words, Christian theology—the systematic study of God's self-revelation in Jesus Christ and of the human experience, understanding, knowledge, and reception of that revelation, and in particular how Christian disciples are expected to live their lives—can be treated as a thematization of personal experience, as a set of doctrines, as a system of thought, and as a body of knowledge that has developed historically over time. The questions and the differentiations to which they have led—here called the experiential, the doctrinal, the systematic, and the historical—can be listed as follows:

THE FOUR DIFFERENTIATIONS OF THEOLOGY	
COGNITIONAL QUESTION	DIFFERENTIATION IN THEOLOGY
What is the Christian faith about?	Theology as reflection on lived experience
Which is the true faith Christians should profess?	Theology as doctrine
How do the truths of faith fit together and what do they mean?	Theology as a system
What is permanently true in matters of faith, and what is changeable?	Theology as historical

Figure 2

These concerns might be represented schematically as follows:

THE FOUR DIFFERENTIATIONS OF THEOLOGY				
presented schematically				

Figure 2a

Theology as Experience

The phrase "theology as the thematization of lived experience" comes from Terry Tekippe (d. 2005) and his fine introduction to theology titled *Theology: Love's Question* (1991). His point is that theology is an attentive, intelligent, and reasoned reflection on experience, the thematization of the Christian's lived ecclesial experience of Jesus Christ and the Gospel. Christians reflect on their faith in Christ, what it means, and how to live it in daily life, and they articulate their understanding and reflections in writing, music, speech, art, poetry, and other media. In this sense all Christians do theology insofar as they reflect on and attempt to express their Christian faith.

Theology as an account of Christian experience is a continuous feature of ecclesial life and activity. People meditate on the Scriptures, the liturgy, and the sources of their faith. They write about all this and they produce articles and books. Interestingly, the key practitioners have varied from era to era, and their "products" can be said to have varied according to need and intended audience. In the early church the key theologians were the apostles, evangelists, and writers of the New Testament. They reflected on their experience of Christ and wrote it down in order to communicate it to others in forms such as the gospels and epistles. These first writers were followed by a group of sub-apostolic Fathers including Clement of Rome (d. 99) and the author of the *Didache*, an early treatise with instructions on how to live the Christian life, sometimes called *The Teaching of the Twelve Apostles*.

In the second century the principal theologians were the philosophers, thinkers, and apologists who mainly inhabited the eastern Mediterranean. These included Justin Martyr (d. 165) and Tertullian (d. ca. 220). They made a defense (Gk. *apologia*) of their Christian faith against both Judaism and the Roman empire. They tried to show how Christianity was the fulfillment of Judaism and the ancient prophecies, and distinguished the Gospel from the thought and social life of the Roman Empire.

In the patristic period (200–800) the main practitioners of theology became the bishops who preached homilies, taught and catechized the faithful, and defended orthodox beliefs from the challenges of heresy and other misunderstandings. Many of their homilies have been incorporated into the *Office of Readings* in the Liturgy of the Hours.

In the Middle Ages, monks became the principal practitioners of theology. They studied and reflected prayerfully on the Scriptures and also on the homilies of the Fathers. This practice of *lectio divina*, a meditative reading and reflection, gave birth in time to a welter of monastic commentaries on Scripture.

In the High Middle Ages the key theologians were the teachers of the monastic schools ("scholastics"). Some of these schools became Europe's first universities. They endeavored to systematize the scriptural and patristic sources into an overall and coherent account of the Christian faith.

In the Tridentine era, between the Council of Trent (1545–63) and Vatican II (1962–65), the chief theologians were the seminary professors and Catholic university teachers whose primary task was to educate clergy and religious in the doctrines of Catholicism. They taught students how to defend Catholic beliefs from the challenges of the Protestant Reformers. This imbued all Tridentine Catholic thought with an apologetic slant. This polemical slant was also mirrored in the Reformation communities, where the key theologians were the scriptural exegetes, teaching ministers how to interpret the Scriptures properly and how to defend their interpretations against Roman Catholic apologists. However, in the eighteenth and nineteenth centuries both Catholic and Protestant theology began to feel the chill winds of modernity, particularly modern philosophy, modern empirical science, and modern critical scholarship. All these posed radical questions and challenges to Christian faith, especially to its claim to a divine revelation in history. This endowed apologetics in the nineteenth and the first half of the twentieth century, in both Catholic and Protestant or Reformed circles, with an additionally defensive twist.

Today, in the post–Vatican II period, the challenges of modernity and postmodernity are the subject of theology. Theology has become a largely lay-led discipline concerned with the meaning of faith within a secular, pluralist culture. Moreover, the rise of social justice and ecological concerns has challenged theologians to respond to the Marxist jibe that religion is an opium. The emergence of liberation theologies and feminist thought in response attempts to show the relevance of Christianity to a world imbued with inequality, violence, and injustice.

In sum, theology deals with human experience, particularly Christians' lived experience within the social, cultural, and historical context or situation in which they find themselves. Theologians produce books, articles, and other media that are products typical of their time in order to meet the challenges of the time.

Theology as Doctrine

Besides a concern with experience, theology from early on has also had to address the question of truth. There are many and various theological opinions, expressions, and viewpoints, yet when push comes to shove, what is the true, orthodox faith of the church? What do Christians believe for sure? Which is the true belief?

All human beings have a critical faculty of judgment. When viewing, reading, or listening to the claims of another, we ask: Is it so? Is this true? Thus Christians individually and the church as a whole sift the many writings, views, and opinions of theologians. Sometimes in a solemn manner, the church exercises the critical faculty of judgment, determining whether or not the writings under discussion express the true faith of the church. This process can be seen operating informally even within the New Testament, and then within the early church as it dealt with the philosophies and pagan theologies extant in the Roman Empire. This process led in time to the formal emergence of doctrine and dogma as theological features in the life and history of the church. Such doctrine and dogma can be seen in the statements of the early creeds, the symbols and disciplinary decisions of the councils.

This magisterial strand within theology emerged with the first ecumenical council of the church, the First Council of Nicea in 325, although by modern standards it would barely be described as a synod. Nevertheless, the magisterial strand—the need for the church to teach authoritatively what its faith is and to differentiate truth from falsehood—has grown and developed ever since, particularly in the second millennium and in recent times. A glance at a collection of documents and pronouncements such as the Denzinger-Schönmetzer *Enchiridion symbolorum definitionum et declarationum de rebus fidei et morum* or Neuner and Dupuis' *The Christian Faith in the Doctrinal Documents of the Catholic Church* demonstrates this development. Indeed, since Vatican II there have been many magisterial teachings and pronouncements from the pope, the various offices of the Vatican, and synods of bishops. Rarely altogether noncontroversial, the magisterium has dealt with a wide range of topics it deemed in need of clarification or expression if the Christian faithful were to be shielded from error or guided in a certain direction.

So theology, the systematic study of God's self-revelation in Jesus Christ and of the human experience, understanding, knowledge, and reception of this revelation, includes not only an experiential element as noted above but also a normative element. In other words, within theology there is a thematization of lived experience and also doctrine and dogma that express the church's authoritative teaching about what is really and truly what Christians should believe. There is also, as we shall now see, a systematic component.

Theology as System

In the High Middle Ages another differentiation emerged within theology as it became a critical academic discipline. The expanding monastic schools, now emerging as the first universities, began to espouse new pedagogical methods reflecting a mentality that sought to bring order and system to learning and knowledge so as to yield a deeper understanding of the Christian faith and how it was structured.

The issues faced by theologians in the Middle Ages were arguably twofold. First, how did the many and varied truths of the Christian faith fit together? After all, the sources sometimes appeared to be full of contradictions and conflicts. The sayings of Scripture were not always coherent: how might the precept of Jesus in Matthew 5:44 ("love your enemies") be reconciled with what Jesus says later in the same gospel about those who might harm one of the little ones (Matt 18:6: "it would be better for you if a great millstone were fastened around your neck and you were drowned in the depth of the sea")? In much the same way, the sayings of the Fathers appeared to be inconsistent. Cyprian of Carthage (d. 258), for example, insisted that there was no salvation outside the church (*Letters*, lxxii), and this was also the opinion of Augustine and many others, yet Justin Martyr had argued that just as devout Jews could be saved by following the Law of Moses, so those who died before Christ could be saved by following the natural law of goodness written in their hearts (*Trypho*, 45). Furthermore, the sayings of the Fathers appeared at times to contradict the Scriptures. For instance, how might Augustine's somewhat pessimistic view about the fate of unbaptized babies be harmonized with 1 Timothy 2:3-5, which states that God wants all to be saved? The scholastic mentality wanted to reconcile, bring together, and systematize all these real or apparent conflicts in the authorities. The high medieval mind-set was encapsulated by Peter Abelard (d. 1142) in his provocative *Sic et Non* (1120). It was a mentality that raised multiple questions about the number and class of the sacraments and the conditions for receiving them, the fruits of the Holy Spirit, the nature and list of capital sins, the multiple forms of grace, the key works of mercy, and so on. It was prompted more than anything by the new theological method of the *quaestio*, which we will examine in a later chapter.

A second concern in the medieval period was with the moral life and how to reach heaven. How do humans live a good life? What do the truths of faith actually mean for the way men and women should live their lives? The hope of heaven and the fear of hell in an era of short life expectancy lent urgency to the Christian life. Thus many of the questions addressed by Aquinas in the *Summa Theologiae* concern the acquisition of virtue.

This medieval question about the good life and how to live virtuously anticipated in some respects the modern systematic questions about the relationship of religion and theology to culture and everyday living, the meaning of Christian discipleship and how faith and theology might leaven and baptize other domains of human knowledge. In the high medieval period faith infused culture, and yet, once theology began to be differentiated from spirituality and philosophy, the relationship of faith to other domains began to become distinct, then fragmented, and finally compartmentalized. This process was sealed by the new discoveries and directions of science, scholarship, and philosophy after the Enlightenment. In modern times the systematic differentiation within theology raises this issue of the relationship of religion and theology to the natural and human sciences, medicine, the arts, economics, fashion and media, international relations, poverty and injustice, environmental concerns, and all the other diverse domains and issues of contemporary living. What might the doctrines of Christianity say to the modern world? How do Christians express meaningfully the wisdom of the Christian faith in a secular-pluralist world? What in turn might the world, in which the Holy Spirit is at work, be saying to the church? The systematic differentiation in theology, which emerged and developed from the medieval era onward—that is, theology as a system and as a systematized body of knowledge—is crucial today if the meaning of the Christian faith and of religion is to be proclaimed to modern culture.

Theology as Historical

Finally, theology today, which we have argued here is experiential, systematic, and doctrinal, is also historical. Since the eighteenth century and the rise of modern critical scholarship, particularly historical scholarship and the human and social sciences, theologians, although long resistant to the implications of all this, have become increasingly aware that the new or modern world is very different from the world of the Bible, the early church, the Fathers, and the medieval monastics. Moreover, as Christianity spread overseas to the New World, to Asia, and to Africa, cultural diversity was added to historical difference. The issue of historical and cultural awareness is nowadays unremarkable and second nature, but within theology, historical and cultural concerns have made their mark only in relatively recent times. This is an aspect of what Bernard Lonergan and others have called the modern sense of history or "historical consciousness." Modern philosophy reveals the historically and culturally conditioned nature of all truth, thus highlighting the complex relationship between truth and history, permanence and change.

Historical scholarship has had an enormous impact on every domain of twentieth- and twenty-first-century theology. Enormous advances have taken place in the study of the historical sources of theology, notably in Scripture, liturgy, and patristics, and these have powered various renewal movements, furnishing a deeper and richer awareness of the contexts that gave rise to the sources Christians rely on. All areas of theology today are permeated with a historical awareness, arguably absent from the neoscholastic theology that dominated Catholic thought prior to Vatican II. Things were different in the past, and they might be quite different in the future. Historical consciousness thus poses a number of challenges, including an acute awareness of how the church itself, its practices, traditions, and beliefs have changed and developed over time and varied from place to place. How can the Christian faith be the same, true for all time, and yet paradoxically vary, change, and develop? In particular, historical consciousness raises the thorny issue of doctrinal change and development and the need to differentiate what is central from what is peripheral. What is permanently true? What is changeable? For instance, if one pope has stated that women may not be admitted to ordination to the priesthood, is this a permanent truth that binds successor popes, or might things be different again under a different papacy?

Not all Christians are comfortable with recognizing the role of history in theology. Roman Catholicism in general gives this historical differentiation within theology a qualified acceptance. It could be argued that Eastern Orthodoxy gives it a qualified rejection, preferring to inhabit the patristic world. Protestant and Reformed theologies are divided. Some have reacted with an outright rejection of history (evangelicalism and fundamentalism, which seek in different ways to inhabit the world of the Scriptures), others with an open acceptance (liberal Protestantism).

4. The Function of Theology

We began with a series of questions about theology: What is theology? What is it about? What is theology for and what does it seek to do? We now complete our initial exploration by examining the functions of theology and the sources it uses.

Dei Verbum *and the Sources of Theology*

The issue of the sources of Catholic theology has to some extent been authoritatively determined by the magisterial pronouncements of the Second Vatican Council in its Dogmatic Constitution on Divine Revelation, *Dei Verbum*. Other teaching is contained in the council's Constitution on the Sacred Liturgy, *Sacrosanctum Concilium*, and the Pastoral Constitution on the Church in the Modern World, *Gaudium et Spes*. All these documents build on previous statements of the magisterium, especially those of the Council of Trent. They have established important and arguably definitive parameters for subsequent Catholic theology, although these have not been universally accepted or always appropriated by individual theologians.

The teaching of Vatican II might be summed up as follows. *Dei Verbum* 2–6 stated that Jesus Christ is the mediator of revelation and at the same time the fullness of revelation (2). The "Mediator is the message," we might say.

> Jesus . . . completed and perfected Revelation and confirmed it with divine guarantees. He did this by the total fact of his presence and self-manifestation—by words and works, signs and miracles, but above all by his death and glorious resurrection from the dead, and finally by sending the Spirit of truth. . . . The Christian economy, therefore, since it is the new and definitive covenant, will never pass away; and no new public revelation is to be expected before the glorious manifestation of our Lord, Jesus Christ. (*Dei Verbum* 4)

Dei Verbum 7–10 then outlined what in effect are the primary sources of the revelation given in Jesus Christ, namely, the Bible, the tradition of the church (the church's teaching, customs and practices, life and people, the sacred liturgy, and the witness of the saints), and the teachings of the magisterium, this last being at the service of the Word of God expressed in Scripture and tradition. This triadal relationship between Scripture, tradition, and magisterium, proposed by the council and based on the previous teaching of the councils of Trent and Vatican I but developed much more extensively in *Dei Verbum*, mediates to believers today the teaching revealed by Christ. Scripture, tradition, and the church's magisterium, therefore, in the vision of *Dei Verbum*, form the primary media of revelation and the primary sources for theological reflection.

The triad of Scripture-tradition-magisterium, however, must be contextualized within the whole life of the church. It is the church in its totality that manifests and mediates the person of Jesus Christ, his teaching, life, and grace to the world today. According to the council's Constitution on the Sacred Liturgy, *Sacrosanctum Concilium* (1963), the place par excellence where that takes place is in the liturgy (10), which is the work of Christ the high priest (7):

> From the liturgy, therefore, and especially from the Eucharist, grace is poured forth upon us as from a fountain, and the sanctification of [men and women] in Christ and the glorification of God to which all other activities of the Church are directed, as toward their end, are achieved with maximum effectiveness. (*Sacrosanctum Concilium* 10)

The function of the liturgy in re-presenting Christ is not developed in *Dei Verbum* but is treated implicitly as part of tradition (8). Moreover, *Dei Verbum* does not discuss what might be termed the "secondary sources" of revelation, which are treated *passim* in *Gaudium et Spes*. These secondary sources are essentially creation and history, that is, everything else and every other medium that may be a vehicle of God's self-communication, including personal experience, the thoughts and opinions of others, the understanding of the created order as willed and sustained by God, the beauty of nature and the universe, the events of history, the signs of the times, benevolent social movements such as those for international development, changes to the political world order, and so on. These secondary sources might also include the other world religions since they often mediate aspects of revelation that make more explicit the message given in the primary sources of Scripture, tradition, and magisterium. However, because the Christian faith is founded on the divine revelation given in the historical person of Jesus Christ, who became incarnate, lived, died, and rose from the dead at a particular time and place in history, all these secondary sources, it is argued, are normed by the primary sources (Scripture, tradition, and magisterium).

According to *Dei Verbum*, then, the Bible and the church's tradition, articulated, guarded, preserved, and applied by the magisterium, constitute the primary sources that transmit the content of divine revelation to Christians today. These sources form the basic infrastructure of Catholic theology. It is worth pausing for a moment longer to examine this triad of Scripture-tradition-magisterium, since it gives method and shape to Catholic theology.

The importance of the issue of the sources of theology becomes particularly apparent in ecumenical dialogues. Interestingly, the 1888 Lambeth Conference of the Anglican Communion came close to the future position of Vatican II when it approved the so-called Lambeth Quadrilateral, which articulated the four essential principles for a reunited Christian church: the Scriptures, the creeds (Apostles and Nicene), the two sacraments of baptism and Eucharist, and the historic episcopate. Modern Anglican commentators often speak of the importance of Scripture and tradition, although little of the function of an ecclesiastical magisterium. Liberal Anglican theologians have tended to speak of Scripture, tradition, and right reason or Scripture, tradition, and experience. Evangelical and other Reformed theologians follow the traditional Lutheran stance of *sola scriptura* (Scripture alone), although they would acknowledge traditions of interpretation of the Scriptures or sets of doctrinal principles that regulate how the Bible is to be interpreted.

In all the ecumenical dialogues the same sets of questions can be asked: What is the Bible? Why and how is the Bible authoritative? What is the relationship of the Bible to the church? How can the Bible be applied to modern problems? How is the Bible's meaning to be interpreted authentically? Moreover, every Christian community has traditions, and this leads to a further set of questions: What is tradition? What authority do tradition and the traditions of the churches have? How changeable is tradition in the face of new needs and new questions, such as the ordination of women? Finally, there is a third set of questions: What is the relationship between Scripture and tradition? How are Scripture and tradition related to church authority? How does church authority relate to me, my experience, my personal opinions?

Catholics see in *Dei Verbum* 7–10, the contents of which are neatly summarized and expressed in the *Catechism of the Catholic Church* 80–95, a much-discussed series of authoritative principles that guide theological reflection. According to the Dogmatic Constitution, Scripture, tradition, and the church's magisterium are inextricably linked and necessarily interrelated. Scripture and tradition form a complex unity, the deposit of revelation, and this deposit is entrusted to the church, governed by its pastors and guided by its magisterium. The *Catechism of the Catholic Church* states how Scripture and tradition form a complex unity:

> "Sacred Tradition and Sacred Scripture, then, are bound closely together and communicate one with the other. For both of them, flowing out from the same divine well-spring, come together in some fashion to form one thing and move towards the same goal."* (CCC 80)

This "one thing" of Scripture-and-tradition is entrusted to the church, whose magisterium has the responsibility for authoritatively interpreting it:

> The apostles entrusted the "Sacred deposit" of the faith (the *depositum fidei*),† contained in Sacred Scripture and Tradition, to the whole of the Church. . . .
>
> "The task of giving an authentic interpretation of the Word of God, whether in its written form or in the form of Tradition, has been entrusted to the living, teaching office of the church alone. Its authority in this matter is exercised in the name of Jesus Christ."‡ (CCC 84–85)

The magisterium, however, is not above this deposit in the sense of being in charge of it but is its servant. Like every Christian, those who constitute the members of the magisterium—the pope and bishops, and the priests, deacons and others who collaborate with them—are under the Word, which they are to receive with open faith and trust:

> [The] task of interpretation has been entrusted to the bishops in communion with the successor of Peter, the Bishop of Rome.
>
> "Yet this magisterium is not superior to the Word of God, but is its servant. It teaches only what has been handed on to it. At the divine command and with the help of the Holy Spirit, it listens to

---

* *DV* 9.
† *DV* 10 § 1; cf. *1 Tim* 6:20; *2 Tim* 1:12-14 (Vulg.).
‡ *DV* 10 § 2.

this devotedly, guards it with dedication, and expounds it faithfully. All that it proposes for belief as being divinely revealed is drawn from this single deposit of faith." [*DV* 10 § 2] (CCC 85–86)

Scripture, tradition, and the magisterium are ecclesial and dogmatic realities such that they must necessarily go together: should one "fall," the others fall too.

> "Sacred Tradition, Sacred Scripture, and the Magisterium of the Church are so connected and associated that one of them cannot stand without the others. Working together, each in its own way, under the action of the one Holy Spirit, they all contribute effectively to the salvation of souls." [*DV* 10 § 3] (CCC 95)

From a Catholic perspective the unity of the triad Scripture-tradition-magisterium is self-evident in light of the transmission of the deposit of revelation in the early church. At the risk of oversimplifying a complex historical process, we may say that the New Testament was the product of tradition. In the very early church the apostles and disciples handed on the Good News of Christ orally. Elements of these early oral traditions eventually began to be put into writing between 50 and 110. Presumably, as the eyewitnesses died, there was a need for catechetical tools to systematize the message, and with the distances involved in the mission to the Gentiles, the need to avoid the danger of distorting the message. What became known by the late second century as the New Testament began to coalesce into a collection of Christian writings, even though in the first 200 to 250 years they existed in pockets in different places, with a great fluidity as to how and where different books were used. Scholars suggest that it was only in the early third century that the present twenty-seven-book corpus became universally stable.

It is noteworthy that many of the fourth-century councils and synods issued lists of the books of Scripture they used in the liturgy and deemed canonical. In other words, they believed they had the authority to establish the canon of Scripture (*kanōn*, lit. a rod, limit, rule, principle), that is, the commonly agreed content or set of books. Yet, as Jared Wicks, SJ (b. 1929) has argued, once that canon of books had been established, the Scriptures themselves henceforth "ruled" the church and its subsequent development. In other words, once the Bible was treated by Christians as normative, the later church submitted itself to it as a kind of instrument that kept the church faithful through history to the original revelation in Christ and the original experience of the apostles. Tradition therefore had given rise to the Bible and the members of the church wrote it, but later the practice and authority of the church established which books should be included or excluded.

The first serious challenge to the belief that the Bible, the tradition, and the church were intrinsically and reciprocally interrelated occurred during the Reformation. Despite the decadence of the church during the late fifteenth and early sixteenth centuries, this was a period of renewal in biblical scholarship. Far-reaching and complex questions began to be posed about where certain doctrines and ecclesiastical practices, not explicitly mentioned in the Bible, had originated. For instance, where did the Bible speak of purgatory, the use of indulgences, the sacrifice of the Mass, the power of the pope, or the intercession of the saints? Many Catholic theologians at the time justified these beliefs and practices by appealing to oral traditions and liturgical customs the apostles had given to the church by word of mouth. They appealed to such texts as John 21:25 ("But there are also many other things that Jesus did; if every one of them were written down, I suppose that the world itself could not contain the books that would be written"). Bishop John Fisher (d. 1535) asserted that the church's teachings were contained partly (*partim*) in the Bible and partly (*partim*) in unwritten apostolic traditions that had been handed down within the church. However, Luther and the Reformers argued that many of these traditions, doctrines, and practices were superstitious. The church had invented them and added them to what is in the Bible. The church had to be purified by a return to the basics, and so Luther rejected the traditional common teaching in favor of Scripture as the only source of revelation (*sola scriptura*). The Bible alone, in his view, contained everything necessary for our salvation. Johann Eck (d. 1543), who tried to rally the Catholic forces against Luther, argued that the church was a reality more fundamental than the Scriptures. The Bible could only be understood within an ecclesial context. It was not self-interpreting; there were many disputed issues and such problems needed a divinely mandated authority to deliberate and establish the correct interpretation.

Many of Eck's arguments were echoed by the Council of Trent, which stated:

> [The] Gospel is contained in the written books and unwritten traditions which have come down to us, having been received by the apostles from the mouth of Christ himself or from the apostles by the dictation of the Holy Spirit, and have been transmitted as it were from hand to hand. (Council of Trent, *Decree of Reception of the Sacred Books and Apostolic Traditions* DS 1501/ND 210)

Trent then added that the only authentic and authoritative interpreter of the Bible was the church and anyone reading the Bible must do so without conflict with the traditional understanding (DS 1507). Note that the council here was speaking of the Gospel as a primary reality before its written expression. Note too the council's carefully worded formula that the Gospel was handed down "in written books and unwritten traditions." This statement was in fact a compromise. The draft version of the text used the phrase *partim . . . partim* but the council fathers settled for *et*: the Gospel had been transmitted through both written books and unwritten traditions. Nevertheless, thanks to the Counter-Reformation catechesis of Peter Canisius (d. 1597), Robert Bellarmine (d. 1621), and others, the *partim . . . partim* formula gained ascendancy. If a doctrine such as purgatory could not be found in the Bible, it must have come from an unwritten apostolic tradition. Indeed, in the nineteenth century some Catholic theologians even espoused the view that the Gospel was contained entirely in tradition and only partly in Scripture (*totaliter-partim*).

This debate was given new impetus in the mid-twentieth century, in the period of theological ferment following the solemn definition in 1950 by Pope Pius XII of the dogma of the assumption (that the Blessed Virgin Mary at the end of her earthly life was assumed body and soul into heaven). While many would acknowledge that doctrines not explicitly found in the Bible, such as the Trinity or the two natures of Christ, were more or less implicitly contained therein, where was Mary's assumption? Moreover, in this case even tradition was not free from difficulty. Was the only basis for this doctrine, therefore, the widespread popular devotion of the faithful, now definitized by an act of papal authority?

Dei Verbum, which underwent several major revisions before it was promulgated in 1965, settled few of these disputed issues. In fact, the more innovative theologians of the 1950s and the Vatican II period such as Joseph Ratzinger (b. 1927), Yves Congar (d. 1995), Karl Rahner (d. 1984), and Henri de Lubac (d. 1991) subscribed to the view that all the doctrines necessary for salvation were contained implicitly in Scripture, although Scripture and tradition should be read together to be certain. But like the Council of Trent previously, *Dei Verbum* seems to sidestep the dispute about the dogmatic content of Scripture and tradition, preferring to speak instead of their integral and reciprocal connection: they both come from "one and the same divine well-spring," form "one thing," and move toward the same goal (*Dei Verbum* 9: cf. CCC 80).

The relationship of Scripture, tradition, and magisterium is a lively issue relevant not only to Catholic but to all Christian theology. It is also an interreligious issue in that it raises the question of the status of sacred literature, traditions, and authority within any religion. *Dei Verbum* has undoubtedly been significant in its effect on the church's pastoral life. The Constitution called for a renewed focus on the Bible in the life of the church, and this was widely taken up. A biblical revolution has occurred with effects in every quarter, from parish liturgy and prayer groups to socioeconomic applications of Scripture in religious communities. Meanwhile, the concept of tradition continues to be vibrantly debated in the new questions arising (e.g., gender issues), while the rampant pluralism of contemporary theology has raised the thorny issue of changing traditions. Finally, today perhaps more than any other communion the modern Roman Catholic Church has become a veritable archipelago of differing liturgies, customs, languages, and theological perspectives, and this in turn has raised profound and far-reaching issues for the exercise of the church's magisterium.

St. Anselm's Definition of Theology

When theology was loosely defined above as the systematic study of God's self-revelation in Jesus Christ and of the human experience, understanding, knowledge, and reception of this revelation, and in particular of how Christian disciples are expected to live their lives, we noted that this notion of theology concurred in some respects with the medieval idea. In his *Cur Deus Homo?* (1079), St. Anselm (d. 1109) offered what became the classical definition of theology: *fides quaerens intellectum* ("faith seeking understanding"). What is noticeable in Anselm's definition is that for him theology was something practiced by a person of faith (*fides*). It was an intellectual activity, the desired outcome of which was a greater wisdom or deeper understanding (*quaerens intellectum*) and it presumed both an encounter with objective truth and coherence. For Anselm, in other words, faith and reason worked together in the quest for truth, with reason subordinate to faith. As with any other form of knowledge, theology required an appropriate logical discourse to express itself, which is why Anselm ascribed to philosophy a role as the handmaid of theology, something referred to by Pope John Paul II in *Fides et Ratio* (77).

Anselm's definition has often been used as a helpful starting point for discussing the nature and task of theology. The working definition used here is roughly a descendant of it. Yet, as many point out, this medieval definition has limitations in today's context. Some have argued that its implicit depiction of faith as an intellectual assent to revealed truth is too narrow to express the full reality of theology and the richer, more personalist theology of revelation developed in *Dei Verbum*. Luther, for instance, envisaged faith less as an intellectual activity involving an assent to truth and more as an act of personal trust and confidence in God, a trusting commitment of the heart (*fiducia*, "trust"). Recent theology has taken up these personal and practical dimensions of faith (*fides quaerens actionem*), which are also articulated in the 1992 *Catechism of the Catholic Church*:

> Faith is a personal adherence of the whole man to God who reveals himself. It involves an assent of the intellect and will to the self-revelation God has made through his deeds and words. (CCC 176)

Others have argued that Anselm was making the assumption that the true faith can be known in its content and scope. Today, they say, there is a pluralism of beliefs, with many different churches and other religious systems present. The huge growth in modern critical scholarship has raised complex questions, and so the scope and content of theology are no longer self-evident as they were for Anselm. "The Faith" has itself become a *quaestio disputata* ("disputed question"). Furthermore, could it be said that the marriage of theology with philosophy implied in Anselm's definition is too narrow? Contemporary theology has to dialogue with many other disciplines besides, if it is to express the Christian message adequately and constructively to a world facing many pressing problems, including poverty, women's concerns, environmental issues, and globalization. Theology, therefore, has to engage not only with philosophy but also with the human sciences of anthropology, economics, psychology, and politics, with medicine and the natural sciences. Indeed, there is a two-way exchange, since the human sciences arguably need theology in order to dialogue with human values and to address such essentially human experiences as death, sin, morality, hope, love, and happiness. To give an example: to address guilt, psychology must necessarily intrude upon the domain of moral theology. Where the human sciences circumnavigate or even deny these dimensions of the human being they implicitly espouse reductionist views of being human. Consequently, it could be argued that in order to integrate the human sciences into theology in a coherent and critical manner, a process that de facto is often attempted, we require not merely a new definition of theology, broader than that of St. Anselm, but also a new way of doing theology, a new method.

One thinker who has given explicit and extensive consideration to these problems is Bernard Lonergan. In his *Method in Theology* (1972), Lonergan is said to have gone beyond Anselm in a manner that retains the intellectual dimension Anselm privileges but captures better the raft of activities modern theology is called upon to perform. Lonergan offers a description of theology's function, what it does. For him theology "mediates between a cultural matrix and the significance and role of a religion within that matrix" (*Method in Theology*, xi). This new definition requires some thought, but it would seem to be very helpful for Catholic theology. By describing theology as a mediation between religion and culture Lonergan means essentially an intellectual exchange, but the exchange need not be limited to this, since his account would wish to take seriously all the other dimensions of the human person such as experience, decision, practical action, and love (in older language: the intellect, the will, and the heart). By culture here he meant the meanings and values attached to the social, the social being simply a way of living, the communal patterns of living and operating, such that culture is to society as soul is to body. To define theology, therefore, as a mediation between religion and culture would be to speak of a two-way critical conversation between them. The conversation is not just between faith as a set of truths to be communicated and reason as a set of intellectual activities for receiving and understanding them, but a conversation and exchange at many different levels: head, will, and heart, theory and practice, involving different realms and adapted to differing media.

**THEOLOGY AS A MEDIATION
BETWEEN RELIGION AND CULTURE**

Religion   Culture

Figure 3

For Lonergan the priority would be on the side of religion: in this case the divine revelation given in Jesus Christ. Religion seeks to communicate itself—its reality, traditions, and customs, its values and activities, its meanings, message, and experience—to contemporary culture. Nevertheless, there is also a return movement whereby questions are put to religion by the culture in which it finds itself, and insofar as these are new they become for religion not only a means of becoming incarnate in that culture but also an important driver or motor of development for itself.

Is Theology a Science?

As faith seeking understanding, as a systematic study of God's self-revelation in Christ and the human reception of that revelation, and as a mediation between religion and culture, theology is an intrinsically rational endeavor, an activity involving the use of human reason. But in what manner? How might the rationality of theology be characterized? Could theology be called a science? Or is theology more like an art? Is it a form of critical scholarship, analogous to the study of, say, philosophy or history?

In the *Summa Theologiae*, Aquinas asked the question whether theology was a science. The first objection in this article asserted that theology could not be called a science, because science is said to proceed from human reason, whereas theology proceeds from faith. Aquinas's response to this objection is illuminating:

> I answer that sacred doctrine is a science. We must bear in mind that there are two kinds of sciences. There are some which proceed from a principle known by the natural light of intelligence, such as arithmetic and geometry and the like. There are some which proceed from principles known by the light of a higher science: thus the science of perspective proceeds from principles established by geometry, and music from principles established by arithmetic. So it is that sacred doctrine is a science because it proceeds from principles established by the light of a higher science, namely, the science of God and the blessed. Hence, just as the musician accepts on authority the principles taught him by the mathematician, so sacred science is established on principles revealed by God. (ST I-I, q. 1, a. 2)

For Aquinas, theology was a science. Based on Aristotle's definition of science, it was a science derived from a higher science, in this case divine revelation. Aquinas used the term *scientia* here to mean literally "knowledge." In other words, the knowledge that theology is derived from is the knowledge revealed by God. Moreover, it should be noted that what we translate as "theology" was actually for him part of the broader notion of *sacra doctrina* (lit. sacred teaching, or teaching about sacred things) rather than theology in the more technical or academic sense used today. Nevertheless, Aquinas's point remains: since science can be any knowledge methodically derived from first principles, either lower (dependent on others) or higher (in this case, revelation), theology, a systematized body of knowledge, is a science.

However, since the seventeenth century a new notion of science has arisen. The new science is based on a method that traces its origins to Francis Bacon (d. 1626). In his *Novum Organum* (1620), Bacon proposed that the philosopher, rather than using deductive syllogisms to interpret nature, should instead proceed by freeing his or her mind from all presuppositions, notions, or tendencies that might determine or distort the truth; he or she should employ inductive reasoning, starting from "the facts" and proceeding to a hypothetical axiom that may then be proven and declared a law. This new scientific method therefore was based on induction, its knowledge derived "from the bottom up" through the observation of data, the postulation of hypotheses, and their verification by experiment. By contrast, for Aristotle science was deductive, that is, derived "from the top down," often syllogistically from higher principles.

Moreover, besides being inductive, modern science, unlike its classical and medieval predecessors, is also empirical, that is, it consciously restricts the data permitted to sense data and to what is measurable. Interestingly, Bacon was himself a religious believer, yet while he envisaged philosophy to be rational because it was based on reason, he saw religion as not rational because it relied on faith in revelation.

Since the eighteenth century these new inductive and empirical methods have been applied not only to the natural sciences and mathematics but also to the study of human phenomena. This has given rise to the human sciences of politics, anthropology, cultural studies, sociology, psychology, and economics, which mimic the natural sciences and use the same methods. While it is true that in the last hundred years science itself has undergone a paradigm shift from the cast-iron laws and necessity of Newtonian physics to quantum mechanics, statistical probabilities, and verifiable possibilities, induction and empirical observation are still central characteristics.

The modern sciences originally defined themselves over and against God and theology. They proposed beginning with facts, that is, eschewing all theological or other presuppositions. In this process they explicitly excluded the data of divine revelation. In other words, the empirical method systematically limits the field or range of admissible data to the data of sense, to what can be demonstrated by observation and measurable statistics. Consequently, God can never be the object of the empirical sciences. God is not another object in the world like other objects. The nearest the empirical sciences can come to religion is when the human sciences such as religious studies or psychology focus on the role of religion and study its functioning in a culture or an individual. These human sciences operate, of course, only from the outside, treating religion as an observable phenomenon. They cannot interpret or assess the actual experience of religion or its essence and truth claims.

Besides the data of revelation, the natural and human sciences also either exclude or generally circumscribe the "data of consciousness," the inner personal world of experiences, feelings, memories, images, likes and dislikes, personal choices and decisions. This inner world is expressed especially in human intersubjectivity, symbols, art, music, poetry, literature, language, ways of life, and religion. The empirical sciences are unable to explain love, hate, peace, joy, happiness, beauty, and all interior and personal elements of human individual and communal experience except in their statistical, biological, and psychological antecedents, conditions, trends, principles, and occurrences. True, the human sciences might be able to help diagnose problems and propose remedies or suggest more effective manners of conduct and interpersonal relations, yet they do so always from the outside as treating observable and empirically measurable personal or social phenomena. They cannot interpret, assess, or evaluate the personal experience itself. These "from within" or interior elements of human, personal, and communal experience are not data of sense in the empirical order but rather internal or personal data of consciousness.

However, besides empirical science, mention should be made of critical scholarship, which has come to the fore since the nineteenth century. Scholarship might be said to comprise such domains as philosophy, history, literature, the study of art and music, exegesis, and so on. A scientist might also, of course, be a scholar, applying the principles of contemporary natural and human sciences to, say, an understanding of ancient history, and a scholar might also be a scientist, drawing on historical knowledge to enrich a contemporary theory. Scholarship does deal with such personal and inner data of consciousness, and the scholar is the one expertly able to categorize, discuss, compare, and assess such domains, developing an intimate knowledge of the meanings, intentions, and values of different people from other times and places. Unlike the sciences, scholarship does not generally seek to reach hard and fast principles and laws, but rather to understand the meaning or intention, the truth and falsehood, the right or wrong of particular statements, trends, and actions.

Theology is not a science in the sense of an empirical science because it does not circumscribe its data in the way the empirical sciences do. However, theology is similar to the empirical sciences in that it is rational discourse methodically developed. Without limiting itself to the data of sense or the data of consciousness, it nevertheless uses human reason with all its native capabilities. Moreover, like the modern human and natural sciences, theology too is scientific in that it adopts methods based on the self-same cognitional operations the empirical sciences are based on: data-hypothesis-verification, while adding to this a method for evaluation. Its methodology, as we shall see later, can be inductive, as a reflection on the data of consciousness and experience, but it can also be deductive, as faith seeking understanding.

Theology is most similar to critical scholarship: for example, philosophy and history. Like all scholarly endeavors it has its own mode of discourse, a technical terminology, and methods of demonstration. It endeavors to relate itself ultimately to the data of consciousness and to internal, personal realities. Together with research and interpretation, it also includes judgment and evaluation.

But unlike both empirical science and critical scholarship, theology has as its specific focus the data of divine revelation: God, the revelation of Christ, being a religious person and a member of a religious community. This data is communicated partly as an "outer word," that is, through the transmission of certain historical data about Christ and his teaching, and partly as an "inner Word," that is, through the internal religious experience of the presence and action of the Holy Spirit, making a person capable of hearing and open to the Gospel. The data of revelation—the gift of faith—broaden, deepen, and transfigure human horizons. Beyond both science and scholarship, and without losing the rationality of both, theology views the data of sense and the data of consciousness in relation to—as shot through with—divine revelation. Faith is the "added extra" that makes theology transcend the worlds the empirical sciences study and the worlds critical scholarship studies, to study human beings in their relationship to God. It is this realm of faith that gives theology its specificity (see figure 4) and makes it *sui generis*, unique. Theology, it could be argued, "sublates" or subsumes both science and scholarship and becomes in itself the most general and comprehensive, the most profound and fundamental of all studies.

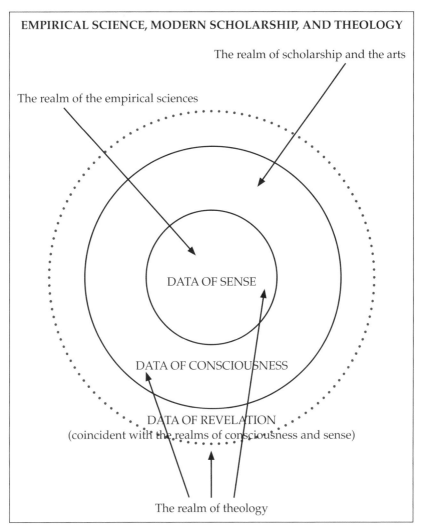

Figure 4

RECENT CATHOLIC THEOLOGY:
SELECT FEATURES AND TRENDS

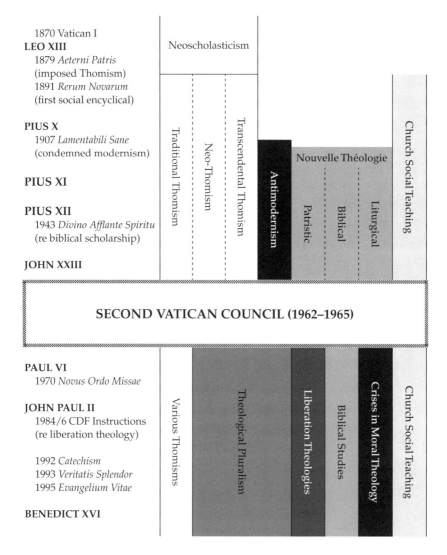

Figure 5

Chapter Two

Recent Theology

In this chapter we draw closer to our topic, the influence of contemporary philosophies on theology, by examining the general trends and developments in theology in the period leading to and from the Second Vatican Council (1962–65). The aim is to offer readers a systematic overview, sketching the historical context within which we will consider, in the next part, the influence of this or that school of philosophy. To make the task manageable we have generally limited ourselves to Catholic theology. To gain a more complete picture, readers would need to acquaint themselves with some of the overlapping trends and convergences in Protestant, Reformed, and Orthodox theology over the same period.

Undoubtedly the key event for recent Roman Catholic thought has been the Second Vatican Council (see figure 5). All the great theologians of the last century were in some way involved with it: Yves Congar, Edward Schillebeeckx, Henri de Lubac, Karl Rahner, Bernard Lonergan, Hans Urs von Balthasar, Hans Küng, Karol Wojtyla (later Pope John Paul II), and Joseph Ratzinger (later Pope Benedict XVI). The council, with the trajectories leading up to it and flowing from it, has undoubtedly occasioned one of the most vibrant periods ever in Catholic, and indeed all Christian, theology. Although closely related to the impressive scientific and technological advances of the period, the striking social and historical upheavals of the mid-twentieth century, the struggle between competing world politico-economic ideologies, and the aftermath of two devastating global wars, Vatican II has often been hailed as "the" religious event of the twentieth century. It was preceded by and itself initiated a process of radical philosophical and theological renewal that has resulted in today's pervasive theological pluralism—a variety of different positions coexisting, with no one being dominant—as well as intense specialization, change, and development.

The current postconciliar situation within the church is marked by strong elements of polarization. Contention usually revolves around one or all of three key issues: church governance, liturgy, and sexual morality. A canon of dissent is often heard, calling on the church to abandon its traditional teaching against abortion and artificial means of contraception, to allow divorcees to remarry in the church, to change its doctrine on homosexual union, to ordain women to the priesthood, to make celibacy optional, to allow Roman Catholics to receive communion at non-Roman Catholic Eucharists, to decentralize and restructure the Roman curia, and to change the style of the papacy and the exercise of ecclesial authority. Commentators frequently refer to ruptures, dislocations, and fragmentation between conservatives and progressives, lay and clerical theologies, theologians and the Vatican, biblical exegetes and parish catechists, theorists and pastors, the academic and the spiritual.

The aim of this part, however, is to avoid the particularities of these divisive issues and to concentrate on the deeper and longer-term developments that have been taking place. It can be argued that the chief shift in theology that occurred with Vatican II was the overthrow of neoscholasticism and its ahistorical and universalist worldview in favor of approaches to theology that take seriously the modern world, culture, and historicity.

In a 1968 essay, "Theology and Man's Future," Bernard Lonergan listed developments in five fields that were profoundly affecting Catholic theology at the time. These were historical scholarship (the impact on theology of the new historical-critical methods of scriptural exegesis together with an awareness of the historical evolution of doctrine); developments in philosophy (especially the new pluralism of philosophies now in use by theologians); the impact of comparative religion, religious studies, and the human sciences such as psychology, economics, sociology, cultural anthropology (with all of which theology was now newly in dialogue); methodologies (as theology shifted from its former Aristotelian-Thomist categories to new critical and hermeneutical approaches); and issues to do with pastoral communications (especially the awareness of the need to adapt to shifting cultural realities and the emergence of new media). Developments in all of these fields have led to a much greater specialization within theology as well as to a greater pluralism. Thomism has largely been superseded by a welter of differing philosophies. A dialogue with other disciplines is under way. Culturally driven concerns such as feminism, liberation, and ecology have entered theology. The impact of global communications and the internet have lent immediacy and urgency to a new atmosphere that is at once ecumenical, interreligious, and dialogical. The chief approach is no longer closure to the world, but openness linked to a renewed desire to engage in evangelization. While what Lonergan said in 1968 might need to be modulated for today, almost half a century later, in a postmodern world of globalization, terroristic threats, and environmental concerns, much of what he outlined still remains current.

If the chief theme of nineteenth-century Catholic theology was the relationship between faith and reason, culminating in the statement of Vatican I in *Dei Filius*, the chief theme of twentieth- and twenty-first-century Catholic theology is the relationship between history and theology. This came to the fore at Vatican II and in its subsequent unfinished agenda, and it can be seen in the various strands of thought that make up the present context. Here we explore that context and select seven features for consideration: neoscholasticism, antimodernism, social teaching, the *Nouvelle Théologie*, the "event" of Vatican II, liberation theology, and the present crisis in moral theology. Figure 5 graphically summarizes the various trajectories of thought.

1. Neoscholasticism

Scholasticism (lit. "of the schools") was the system of philosophy and theology developed in the medieval schools. It was a diverse and broad stream of thought that incorporated into itself the words of Scripture, the sayings of the church Fathers, the wisdom of the ancient classical world, the insights of Augustine and neo-Platonism, and the metaphysics of Aristotle. It developed its own technical language and methodology and became the repository of classical philosophy and the Catholic theological tradition. It prided itself on logic and order and sought to integrate all its knowledge into an overarching synthesis. In the Middle Ages it included a distinctive stream of Platonizing and mystical thinkers such as Hugh of St. Victor (d. 1141), William of St. Thierry (d. 1148), Bernard of Clairvaux (d. 1153), Richard of St. Victor (d. 1173), and Bonaventure (d. 1274). But at its heart was Aquinas's own synthesis and exposition along Aristotelian lines, given above all in the *Summa Contra Gentiles* and the *Summa Theologiae*. Aquinas's heritage was Thomism, a broad tradition of philosophy and theology done according to the mind of Aquinas.

Thomism gradually pervaded the whole scholastic synthesis and became the dominant thread.

Scholasticism passed through three distinctive periods: medieval, renaissance/baroque, and modern. Scholasticism originated in the medieval period and was succeeded by a Second Thomism of the Spanish Counter-Reformation era, sometimes called "baroque scholasticism" or Suarezianism after the great Jesuit theologian and commentator on Aquinas, Francisco de Suárez (d. 1617). The third period, with which we will be concerned here, was that of the nineteenth and twentieth centuries. This was the period of neoscholasticism, associated with the encyclical letter *Aeterni Patris* (1879) of Pope Leo XIII.

Neoscholasticism was an attempt to revive Thomism and the traditions of the medieval university for the modern era. It sought order and clarity. It emphasized metaphysics (the objects of faith and contents of revelation) rather than epistemology (how humans come to know God and faith as a response to God). This, of course, was a trajectory contrary to that followed by most nineteenth- and twentieth-century Western philosophy. In *Aeterni Patris*, Leo XIII called for a return to the "perennial philosophy" as a defense of the faith against the skepticism and subjectivism of the age, but also as a therapy for modernity. Scholasticism was juridically imposed as the official philosophico-theological approach to be used in all Roman Catholic universities and seminaries, and at the heart of this proposal was a renewed study of Aquinas. This was the first time ever that one particular school of thought, however diverse and broad, was made normative within the church. Leo XIII wanted a return to the wisdom of the ancients in order to defend the church from the dangers and threats of modern philosophy, especially its perceived subjectivism and skepticism. More positively, he desired to engage with modern European thought so that it could be corrected with the Gospel of Christ.

Later, at the height of the modernist crisis, Pius X in *Doctoris Angelici* (1914) reinforced Leo's provisions. The Congregation of Studies issued *Twenty-Four Thomistic Theses*, philosophical doctrines that had to be incorporated into every curriculum of philosophy. They rejected any appeal to experience and history and demanded a concern with "truth." The theses covered the key elements of metaphysics, cosmology, epistemology, and natural theology.

Neoscholasticism and the revival of Thomism in the period up to Vatican II could be said to have taken three main forms, which became increasingly discrete and internally sundered: traditional Thomism, neo-Thomism, and transcendental Thomism.

Traditional Thomism was usually taught in seminaries and universities by way of theses, such as those of the classic textbook *Elementa Philosophiae Aristotelico-Thomisticae* (1909) by the Benedictine scholar Joseph Gredt (d. 1939), or *De Verbo Incarnato* (1892) and other tracts on systematic theology by the French Jesuit Louis Billot (d. 1931). One of the greatest exponents of traditional Thomism in this period was the controversial Dominican scholar Reginald Garrigou-Lagrange (d. 1964), lecturer at the Angelicum and supervisor of the doctorates of both Marie-Dominique Chenu (see below) and Karol Wojtyla. For Garrigou-Lagrange and his followers, Aquinas's *Summa* was unsurpassed and unsurpassable. His *La Synthèse Thomiste* (1946) argued against agnosticism, evolutionism, and modern German philosophy by confronting them with Thomistic metaphysics. Without the latter, he argued, Catholic doctrine would ultimately be subverted.

On the other hand, the first half of the twentieth century also saw much new historical research, especially in France and in Toronto, on the writings and thought of Aquinas himself. Thus the work of the Dominican scholar Ambrose Gardeil (d. 1931) and the medievalist Etienne Gilson (d. 1978), author of *Le Thomisme: Introduction au Système de Saint Thomas* (1919), espoused a historical, "back to the texts" approach that sought to renew Thomist thought from within by identifying accretions and eschewing the various corruptions that over time had crept into the tradition. The aim was to explore the thought of Thomas in greater depth within its original context in order to expound its brilliance.

Another more historical-contextual researcher was the French Dominican Marie-Dominique Chenu (d. 1990). He sought to situate the thought of Aquinas within its historical context and Thomas's own spirituality. More a historian than a metaphysician, Chenu took a very different approach from Garrigou-Lagrange. His *Introduction à L'Étude de S. Thomas D'Aquin* (1951) sought to retrieve the patristic sources of Aquinas's thought in Augustine and Denis and to highlight the dramatic history of the *Summa* itself, the Platonizing strands as well as its religious piety. Falling foul of his superiors, he became involved with the worker-priest movements of the 1950s. He was an early exponent of the need to reflect on the "signs of the times." Nevertheless, he became a *peritus* (a theological expert and adviser) at Vatican II and helped write the Pastoral Constitution on the Church in the Modern World, *Gaudium et Spes*. Chenu was an important influence on a number of subsequent Thomistic thinkers such as Jean-Pierre Torrell, the French Dominican and member of the Leonine Commission that is still at work on the definitive texts of

Aquinas; Gregory Rocca (b. 1949); Matthew Levering (b. 1971); and the moral theologian Servais Pinckaers (d. 2008), author of the monumental *The Sources of Christian Ethics* (1995).

The second strand might be called neo-Thomism. These more speculative thinkers attempted an open Thomism, willing to engage in dialogue with twentieth-century science, art, and scholarship, and even to assimilate aspects of modern thought. This more open Thomism was particularly espoused at the University of Louvain under the patronage of Cardinal Désiré-Joseph Mercier of Malines (d. 1926). There Jacques Maritain (d. 1973), one of the greatest Thomist philosophers of the twentieth century, the author of over sixty books, a former member of the *Action Française* movement, a married man and a convert, attempted a critical conversation with political theory, exploring the moral foundations of democracy. Another professor at Louvain was Dominicus de Petter (d. 1971), who attempted a dialogue between Aquinas, personalism, and phenomenology. The young Edward Schillebeeckx was taught by de Petter. Schillebeeckx began from the same historical-contextual approach to Aquinas as Chenu, but also read Edmund Husserl, Maurice Merleau-Ponty, and Martin Heidegger. Interested in the relationship between faith and culture, he taught dogma at the University of Nijmegen beginning in 1958. However, dissatisfied with the pace of change and renewal after Vatican II and under the influence of hermeneutical philosophies, he later abandoned Thomism altogether and began exploring the perplexing link between experience and interpretation in biblical studies. The outcome was his controversial trilogy: *Jesus: An Experiment in Christology* (1979), *Christ: The Christian Experience in the Modern World* (1980), and *The Church with a Human Face* (1985).

This more open form of Thomism is also evident in other thinkers of the period. Mention might be made of the creative and prolific German philosopher Josef Pieper (d. 1997), who in his *The End of Time* (1954) attempted a philosophy of history using elements from Aquinas and the classical tradition.

A third strand was transcendental Thomism, also associated with Louvain. Those who espoused this approach argued that Immanuel Kant's trajectory was not incompatible with the thought of Aquinas, and that epistemology (a concern with human knowing and faith) could be considered prior to metaphysics (a concern with doctrine). This brand of Thomism tried to retrieve the psychological and epistemological elements of Aquinas while taking seriously the challenge of Kant, by studying in particular the so-called transcendental structures of the human person. After all, they said, one had to face the fact that much of the thought of the modern world, its science and technology as well as its philosophy, had been influenced by Kant. Two of the key figures were Joseph Maréchal (d. 1944), a Belgian Jesuit who wrote the five-volume *Departure Point of Metaphysics*, and Maurice Blondel (d. 1949), the French philosopher and professor at Paris and author of *L'Action* (1893). Later exponents, each in his own way, included Emerich Coreth (d. 2006) from Innsbruck; Otto Muck (b. 1928), author of *The Transcendental Method* (1968); Karl Rahner (see below); and Bernard Lonergan. The transcendental approach was also an important influence on the young Karol Wojtyla. When the future Pope John Paul II first began studying the classic theses of Thomistic metaphysics he almost wept at their apparent impenetrability, until helped by a book by Kazimierz Wais (d. 1934), who had tried to rethink the thought of Aquinas in the light of Kant.

Since Vatican II scholasticism in general and Thomism in particular, although still extant today, have been considerably eclipsed and reconfigured. By the 1950s the various schools of Thomism had become increasingly fragmented and disputatious. Unresolved tensions became submerged during the council. They divide those who espouse a pure "back to the sources" Thomism from those who favor a more "open Thomism" engaged with other philosophies.

Meanwhile, in the 1970s and 1980s, theologians began to adopt a wide variety of other philosophies, new approaches, and a more historical and scriptural style. Scholasticism seemed too static and intellectualist, too theocentric and insufficiently anthropocentric to address the needs of the modern person as a developing being with feelings, needs, and practical aspirations. For others, Thomism's lack of an effective philosophical account of the economic, social, cultural, and political dimensions of the human being rendered it alien and inimical to the post-Enlightenment liberal tradition of secular humanism. On the other hand, precisely as a reaction to that tradition, the classical philosophy did offer a sharply contoured alternative to modernity. It thus became for minority groups, such as the thinkers associated with so-called radical orthodoxy (see below), as well as for more traditionally minded Roman Catholics, a means of eschewing modernity and taking refuge in premodern thought.

Presently, in the early twenty-first century, interest in Aquinas, and in scholastic and medieval philosophy in general, is undergoing something of a revival in Catholic seminaries and universities. This is in part a response to John Paul II's *Fides et Ratio* and its attempted rekindling of philosophy. In any case, Thomism continues to form an ongoing point of reference for Catholic thought. Some theologians continue to appeal to Aquinas's account of the virtues for moral theology while others, concerned with analytical, logical, and linguistic issues, reappropriate elements, ideas, and distinctions drawn from him and from other medievals. With the election of Benedict XVI there has been an increased interest in Augustine. Moreover, Thomism and classical philosophy in general are still the quasi-official mode of discourse for magisterial statements, even though most ecclesiastical documents now also adopt biblical, historical, and sociological categories and approaches as well.

2. Antimodernism

A second strand in recent Roman Catholic theology, and one that sometimes appears to be still latent, was the shadow cast by the early-twentieth-century crisis of modernism. Modernism, which Pius X dubbed "a synthesis of all heresies," was more a movement or atmosphere than a clearly defined or systematic set of positions. Modernists argued that the church had to follow the lead given by liberal Protestant thought in order to modernize itself, that is, to take on board the insights of the latest scholarship and scientific discovery. Modernism rejected metaphysics (a rational basis for belief in God) and the supernatural, and deemed faith to be uniquely interior, a motion of the heart, a quality or feeling for the Divine that is ultimately inexpressible in dogmatic definitions and based principally on personal conviction. It was a disparate movement, associated in particular with Alfred Loisy (d. 1940), priest and biblical scholar. In his *L'Evangile et L'Eglise* (1902), Loisy had stated that for Jesus the coming of the kingdom was unexpectedly delayed; Jesus did not anticipate the church and so "it was the kingdom that was awaited but, alas, the Church which arrived" (111). Modernism is also associated with a number of English-speaking thinkers from the turn of the twentieth century, such as George Tyrrell (d. 1909), an Anglo-Irish convert and Jesuit priest, author of *Christianity at the Crossroads* (1909), and lifelong friend of Sister Maude Petre (d. 1942), who published his biography, *Autobiography and Life of George Tyrrell* (1912); and the layman philosopher Baron Friedrich von Hügel (d. 1925).

Modernism was targeted by the 1907 decree *Lamentabili Sane* from the Holy Office, which listed the condemned propositions, and was also rejected by Pope Pius X in his 1907 Encyclical *Pascendi Dominici Gregis*, which attempted to bring the modernist teachings into one group, pointing out the connections, identifying the root causes, and prescribing remedies. One of the latter was the *Anti-Modernist Oath* (DS 3537-50) to be taken by all seminary professors, teachers, and priests. Watchdog committees were set up in every diocese to combat modernists, and a defensive, witch-hunt atmosphere ensued, suggesting a gathering sense of crisis that became the hallmark of all Roman Catholic theology in the first half of the twentieth century. Even the writings of Cardinal John Henry Newman became doubtful, and for much of the century Newman was read more for his spirituality than for his theology. The antimodernist mentality, moreover, was reinvigorated by Pius XII's encyclical letter *Humani Generis* (1950), a sort of new *Syllabus of Errors*, which dealt with certain forms of philosophical existentialism, the social sciences, and erroneous views of creation (DS 3875-83). After the Second World War, however, the liturgical, biblical and patristic renewal movements began to assert their presence. With the announcement of Vatican II by John XXIII in 1959 and the consequent "opening of the windows," some of the darker antimodernist clouds began to disperse. Nevertheless, even in the late 1950s some of the more innovative theologians associated with the *Nouvelle Théologie*, such as Henri de Lubac, continued to be under official scrutiny.

The need for clarity in Catholic doctrine remains perennially important for the church, especially given the challenges of scholarship. The present situation is one of a greater openness and willingness to dialogue. On the other hand, many of the questions raised by the modernists remain unanswered. For instance, why and how does doctrine change? Who were the real authors of the Scriptures? Did the miracles of Jesus really occur? How realistically should the texts of Genesis, or the Old Testament in general, be read? What can behavioral psychology teach Christians?

3. Social Teaching

One of the most important features of recent Catholic theology—in itself a fascinating instance of doctrinal development—has been the emergence of a large and comprehensive body of papal, conciliar, and synodal teaching on political, social, economic, and international matters. The first acknowledged social encyclical was Leo XIII's *Rerum Novarum* ("Of New Things") in 1891, which ever since has set the agenda for magisterial teaching on social matters. It analyzed the social conditions of the late nineteenth century stemming from the Industrial Revolution, condemning socialism and class division but defending the right of workers to form trade unions. Interestingly, Leo's emphasis on the rights of workers and their entitlement to just remuneration marked a significant change from what was perceived to be the church's then-usual socio-political alignment with the aristocracy. *Rerum Novarum* was followed in time by three other papal pronouncements: Pius XI's *Quadragesimo Anno* (1931), on the reconstruction of the social order, which critiqued both capitalism and communism; John XXIII's *Mater et Magistra* (1961), on the need to provide for the temporal conditions of humanity as well as the spiritual; and the latter's *Pacem in Terris* (1963), which dealt with disarmament, the international order, the conditions for peace, the need to work for the common good, and human rights and responsibilities. In this last, John XXIII clearly states that "peace on earth, which all people of every era have most eagerly yearned for, can be firmly established only if the order laid down by God is dutifully observed" (1). The background was the Cold War, the Cuban missile crisis, and the threat of a nuclear holocaust.

Church social teaching falls into two periods: from 1891 to 1963 and from 1963 to the present. In the first period, from Leo XIII to John XXIII, the style of the teaching was self-evidently structured along philosophical lines, drawing heavily on natural law. Since 1965 church social teaching has been structured much more in terms of biblical and personalist categories. This can be seen especially in the writings of John Paul II and again in Benedict XVI's *Deus Caritas Est* (2005). The shift was already evident in Vatican II's groundbreaking Declaration on Religious Freedom, *Dignitatis Humanae* (1965), one of the principal architects of which was the American Jesuit, John Courtney Murray (d. 1967). Although for much of the 1950s his works had been censured by the Vatican, Murray, as is evident from his *We Hold These Truths: Catholic Reflections on the American Proposition* (1960), had long sought to reconcile Catholicism with the political reality of modern religious pluralism. His argument that freedom of religion was a natural right, which was taken up by *Dignitatis Humanae*, effectively reversing previous official teaching, led to the rupture with Archbishop Marcel-François Lefebvre (d. 1991), founder of the traditionalist Society of St. Pius X (SSPX). New ways of thinking were also evident in Paul VI's encyclical *Populorum Progressio* (1967), which called on the wealthier countries to assist the less developed and by means of international aid to show greater charity for the sake of justice. More recently, we should note the three great social encyclicals of John Paul II: *Laborem Exercens* (1981), which outlined a framework for analyzing sociopolitical questions and offered an extensive theology of human work; *Sollicitudo Rei Socialis* (1987), on Gospel values relating to justice and the preferential love for the poor; and *Centesimus Annus* (1991), which looked back to developments in the hundred years since *Rerum Novarum* and reaffirmed the inalienable dignity of every human person.

4. *La Nouvelle Théologie*

Despite the strongly antimodernist spirit of the early twentieth century and the juridical imposition of Thomism and neoscholasticism, new lines of theological thinking developed in the interwar period in France and Germany. The events of the two world wars caused a massive shift of perspectives for the battered peoples of Europe, and the new theological ideas which then developed formed a remote preparation for Vatican II. *La Nouvelle Théologie* rejected the sterility of scholasticism and espoused more historical, personalist, biblical, and patristic approaches.

In France the new group of theologians included such luminaries as Pierre Teilhard de Chardin (d. 1955), author of *The Phenomenon of Man* (1959). Teilhard, a visionary if complex figure, a paleontologist as well as a theologian, would later in the Vatican II period inspire progressive Catholic thinkers. Other exponents included Gabriel Marcel (d. 1973), the existentialist philosopher, and the Jesuit patristic scholar Jean Daniélou (d. 1974), who wrote his doctorate on Gregory of Nyssa, specialized in ecclesiology and ecumenism, and was a contributor at Vatican II to the draft text of *Lumen Gentium*.

The two greatest new thinkers in France at that time were the Jesuit Henri de Lubac and the Dominican Yves Congar. De Lubac rejected the standard fare of Suarezian Thomism in favor of his own private study of the philosophy of Gilson and Blondel and a deep immersion in patristic and medieval theology, particularly Origen. For him the greatest century was the twelfth, significantly not the thirteenth; it was the era prior to Aquinas, the time of Bernard of Clairvaux, William of St. Thierry, and Rupert of Deutz (d. 1130). De Lubac wrote several foundational works that had a widespread influence on mid-twentieth-century theology, including *Catholicism* (1938), which showed how the phrase "mystical Body of Christ" referred originally to the eucharistic body of the Lord rather than to the church; *Corpus Mysticum* (1939), on the reciprocal relationship between the church and the Eucharist; the highly controversial *Surnaturel: Études Historiques* (1946), which argued for a narrower gap between grace and nature than that conceived of in much of the neoscholastic theology then current; and the highly readable *The Splendor of the Church* (1953), whose structure and content largely anticipated *Lumen Gentium*. His theology stressed the nuptial relationship between the soul and Christ, and also the feminine nature of the church as the Bride of Christ and mother of believers. Although he was under intense suspicion throughout most of the postwar years, de Lubac was rehabilitated at Vatican II and, indeed, helped draft *Dei Verbum*, *Lumen Gentium*, and *Gaudium et Spes*. Moreover, his thought had a profound impact on Hans Urs von Balthasar and Karol Wojtyla.

The other important French theologian of the *Nouvelle Théologie* was Yves Congar, a student of Maritain and Chenu. An extensive writer on the theology of ecumenism, the role of the laity, and the need for reform in the church, he penned notably *Tradition and Traditions* (1960/1984) and the three-volume *I Believe in the Holy Spirit* (1983). At Vatican II he helped draft *Lumen Gentium*, *Dei Verbum*, *Unitatis Redintegratio*, *Ad Gentes*, and *Dignitatis Humanae*. Although he greatly admired Anglicanism, especially its liturgy, he saw more hope of a rapprochement with the churches of the East. After Vatican II he focused on some of the unresolved issues such as reception of doctrine, doctrinal development, and the links between biblical studies and systematic theology.

Meanwhile in Germany, as Edmund Husserl pioneered the new philosophical reflection of phenomenology, a number of his pupils, some high profile, became Catholics, including Max Scheler (d. 1928), Edith Stein (d. 1942), and Dietrich von Hildebrand (d. 1977), and these in turn opened up new avenues for theology. One of the two outstanding German exponents of the *Nouvelle Théologie* was Romano Guardini (d. 1968), who wrote his doctoral dissertation at Freiburg on St. Bonaventure. His writings, which included *The Spirit of the Liturgy* (1918/1937) and *The Faith and Modern Man* (1952), constituted powerful studies of traditional themes in the light of present-day challenges. In *The End of the Modern World* (1956) he argued that humanity had lost its place in the universe because God no longer has a place there. Yet, he added, a new age was coming in which the fight between Christianity and secularism would be sharpened and in which it would be possible to restore human dignity and a sense of place, provided Christians cultivated the virtues of obedience, trust, courage, charity, humility, and asceticism. Guardini assisted the liturgical commission in preparation for Vatican II.

Another important German thinker of the time was Karl Adam (d. 1966), an acclaimed ecclesiologist, patristic scholar, and authority on St. Augustine. His *The Spirit of Catholicism* (1924) was one of the finest introductions to the Catholic faith written in the twentieth century. His writings centered on the need for an understanding of our relationship with Christ himself, with a particular stress on the doctrine of the Mystical Body. This doctrine, he averred, was especially suitable to his time, when people were desperately seeking a principle of unity. Thus "in our day," he asserted, the "Church is coming to birth in people's hearts."

One of the centers of *Nouvelle Théologie* in postwar Germany was the University of Munich, where Joseph Ratzinger studied for the priesthood in the late 1940s. There Ratzinger was introduced through the writings of de Lubac to Augustine and the Fathers. He also imbibed, instead of traditional Thomism, a range of modern philosophers including Friedrich Nietzsche, Martin Heidegger, and Martin Buber. The faculty had a number of notably progressive thinkers, such as the New Testament scholar Friedrich Maier (d. 1957); the systematician Michael Schmaus (d. 1993), who was endeavoring to reconstruct dogmatic theology in the light of the liturgical, patristic, and biblical renewal; and Richard Egenter (b. 1902), who was rethinking moral theology in biblical terms. Gottlieb Söhngen (d. 1971) supervised Ratzinger's doctorate on Augustine and his *Habilitationsschrift* on Bonaventure. At Vatican II, Ratzinger worked with Karl Rahner as an adviser, but after the council—particularly after he resigned his professorship at Tübingen in 1969 because of student unrest and the alleged Marxism of many of the members of the faculty—he found himself increasingly at odds with aspects of Rahner's theology, notably his "anonymous Christian" thesis. Nevertheless, it is interesting to note how Ratzinger's intellectual trajectory gave his writings, especially his *Introduction to Christianity* (1968) and *Principles of Catholic Theology* (1987), a decidedly un-Thomistic and more biblical, historical, and phenomenological slant.

Initially the church's magisterium was cautious toward the *Nouvelle Théologie*, but as a new mood it increasingly fed into a three-pronged renewal of scholarship that paved the way for Vatican II. The advances occurred in biblical, liturgical, and patristic studies. Each of these renewal movements has contributed to the current situation and still largely directs it. Here we will say a brief word about Scripture scholarship and then, still more briefly, a word on the liturgical movement.

New Developments in Biblical Scholarship

The biblical renewal, after a period of official caution, was enthusiastically promoted by the encyclical letter of Pius XII, *Divino Afflante Spiritu* (1943), which boosted Catholic Scripture scholarship and warmly approved the use of historical-critical methods.

Classical exegesis, which can be traced back to Origen (d. 254) and John Cassian (d. 435), presumed that the Bible gave a straightforward, historically factual account of the life and teaching of Jesus. Classical interpretation saw two senses in Scripture, the literal and the spiritual (subdivided into the allegorical, moral, and anagogic senses), which when read together yielded the *sensus plenior* ("fuller sense"). This was the living reading of Scripture within the fullness of revelation and the life of the church (cf. *CCC* 115–18). These classical methods of exegesis were concerned primarily with the meaning of the texts for us; the Scriptures were divine texts containing a human meaning. However, with the rise of rational methods of inquiry in the eighteenth century the classical methods began to be challenged and increasingly replaced, initially within Protestant circles. New historical and literary analyses were applied to the biblical texts, treating them in a neutral manner as literature, with the aim of establishing their original form, analyzing their genre, and identifying the various editing processes that might betray their author's original intention. The purpose was to discover the meaning of the texts in their original context and, by identifying the meaning intended by the human author, to understand the divine intention, that is, the meaning God intended to communicate.

Actually, the first proponent of these new historical-critical methods was a Catholic, the priest and biblical scholar Richard Simon (d. 1712); yet it was not in Catholic but in Lutheran and evangelical domains that the "higher biblical criticism" made initial headway. There the new approaches became mixed up with Enlightenment philosophical positions that stressed the supremacy of human reason, denying *a priori* the possibility of miracles and the supernatural elements of the gospels. The aim was to get behind the supposed myth and dogma of the texts to the "raw historical facts" by clarifying the date, place, author, and author's intention. The method used included textual criticism (establishing the original wording), historical criticism (examining the date, content, and intention of the book, using both internal evidences and such external evidences as archaeology and comparison with nonbiblical literature), form and literary criticism (classifying styles and types of writing such as parables, poetry, history, and prophecy), tradition criticism (tracing the processes involved in the transmission of the oral and written units behind the texts), and redaction criticism (analyzing the motives and intentions of the biblical authors and how they handled the materials at their disposal in order to convey the meaning and message they intended).

One of the early exponents of the new methods was Hermann Samuel Reimarus (1694–1768), who proposed a distinction between the historical Jesus, supposedly a Jewish revolutionary who attempted to establish an earthly messianic kingdom, and the Christ of faith, preached by the church and described in the gospels. According to his posthumously published *Fragmentenstreit* (1778), the disciples stole Christ's body and invented the doctrine of the resurrection. Other similarly revolutionary accounts followed. These led to the famous "Quest for the Historical Jesus," that is, the attempt by scholars in the late nineteenth century to write a historically accurate life of Jesus, using the evidences of all the gospels put together. The presumption behind the Quest was that the biblical texts had been distorted by later church dogma and if this could be peeled back or removed, the historical facts would be revealed. This First Quest was dominated by German exegetes such as David Strauss (d. 1874), Ferdinand Bauer (d. 1860), Adolf von Harnack (d. 1930), and Albert Schweitzer (d. 1965), whose *Quest for the Historical Jesus* (1906) remains a classic. Some English scholars also were involved: see, for instance, *Ecce Homo* (1865) by John Seeley (d. 1895). However, all this scholarship produced widely differing results. Moreover, Karl Barth (d. 1968) later and convincingly argued that the whole project was injurious to Protestant orthodoxy. Was it desirable or even possible to use the biblical sources to write a factual, scholarly scientific history, a history that refused to acknowledge and evaluate the theological nature of the biblical data?

Nevertheless, after World War II a new quest began, led by Rudolf Bultmann (d. 1976), Günther Bornkamm (d. 1990), Ernst Käsemann (d. 1998), and others. Joachim Jeremias (d. 1979), although he distanced himself somewhat from this quest and its hermeneutical presuppositions, in his *New Testament Theology* (1971) sought to establish what were the actual words (*ipsissima verba*) of Jesus himself. British practitioners included Charles H. Dodd (d. 1973) and John Robinson (d. 1983). These "Modern Quest" scholars, like those of the earlier Quest, tended to radicalize the proposed distinction between the historical Jesus and the Christ of faith, endeavoring to separate the real person of Jesus from the dogmatized Christ believed in and preached by the church. The Modern Quest, too, failed to reach consensus.

Since then, some scholars have used approaches and methods that help to contextualize Jesus within the Judaism of his time. The results have often been sensationalist, viewing Jesus as a magician or a liberationist. This Third Quest has been associated with the Jesus Seminar founded in 1985 by Robert Funk (d. 2005), an open skeptic of orthodox Christianity. The Seminar, which comprises over two thousand New Testament exegetes worldwide, including the influential Catholic scholars

John Dominic Crossan (b. 1934) and John P. Meier (b. 1945), often employs controversial methods such as voting on texts and sayings with colored balls: green for *ipsissima verba*, red for redactional additions, yellow for uncertain. On the other hand, the bishop of Durham and biblical scholar N. T. Wright (b. 1948) has argued for a more mainstream Third Quest, one that takes a more self-critical stance, aware of the hermeneutical issues involved and the limitations of historical-critical methods.

Catholic reaction to the new biblical scholarship was initially highly cautious. The new methods and approaches were deemed to have been tainted with nineteenth-century German liberalism. Further, they seemed to treat the scriptural texts as purely human constructions and not as texts of faith within an ecclesial tradition. Moreover, modernism was a warning against reductionist philosophies and theologies that *a priori* demythologize the events and realities of Scripture, reducing them to personal experience or suggesting that the older a text, the more authentic it was—a form of historical positivism. However, during the course of the twentieth century Catholic biblical criticism underwent a transformation such that, after the initial caution, historical-critical methods were increasingly adopted and put into practice. Indeed, they became so acceptable, so revered, so widely used that by the end of the century the magisterium, having encouraged their adoption, now felt it necessary to remind scholars of their limitations.

We can trace three phases in the development of recent Catholic biblical scholarship, each accompanied by a document from the church's magisterium: from Leo XIII's *Providentissimus Deus* in 1893 to 1943, a period of caution; from Pius XII's *Divino Afflante Spiritu* in 1943 to 1993, a positive period; and the present period, inaugurated by the Pontifical Biblical Commission's document *The Interpretation of the Bible in the Church* in 1993.

First, the period from Leo XIII's *Providentissimus Deus* (1893) until 1943 was a time of caution. *Providentissimus Deus* was the magisterium's first treatment of questions raised by modern biblical criticism. The encyclical urged caution. While positive toward the new methods of research, it insisted that there could not be a contradiction between the Word of God traditionally understood and the new findings of scholarship. Leo XIII wished to defend the Scriptures from the rationalism and liberalism of non-Catholic exegesis. He reminded Catholic exegetes that all exegesis must take place within an ecclesial context, that "Catholic doctrine is the norm for interpreting the scriptures" (DS 3283), and that the literal or historical meaning of a text on its own was insufficient. Catholic interpretation, moreover, should draw from tradition and the Fathers of the church. In 1902 the Pontifical Biblical Commission (PBC) was established. Since 1971 it has been subsumed within the Congregation for the Doctrine of the Faith. The PBC was to be a committee of cardinals and consultors to further biblical scholarship and safeguard the authority of the Scriptures. Its statements have never been considered to be *de fide*, but prudential judgments binding on conscience. The PBC at various times has taught that Moses was indeed the author of the Pentateuch (1906), that the Fourth Gospel was historically true (1907), that the book of Genesis contained literal truth (1909), that the Psalms were written by David (1910), and that the first gospel to be written was that of Matthew (1912). Moreover, the Holy Office's 1907 decree *Lamentabili Sane* condemned several modernist articles that related to scriptural exegesis: for example, that "those who believe God is really the author of the scriptures show too much simplicity or ignorance" (DS 3409), that "divine inspiration does not extend to the whole of scripture in such a way that each and every part has been kept free from error" (DS 3411), that "John's narrations are not really historical but a mystical contemplation of the Gospel" (DS 3416), and that "an exegete, provided he does not directly deny the dogmas, is not to be censured when he sets up premises from which it follows that certain dogmas might be historically false or doubtful" (DS 3424).

The second period, from Pius XII's *Divino Afflante Spiritu* (1943) until 1993, was more positive. On the fiftieth anniversary of *Providentissimus Deus*, Pius XII published a landmark encyclical for modern Catholic exegesis. It was in part a reaction to an Italian booklet being circulated at the time warning against modern scholarship and the study of the biblical texts in their original languages. *Divino Afflante Spiritu*, while stressing continuity with previous papal teaching, nonetheless actually strongly encouraged the use of modern historical-critical scholarship, including a knowledge of the biblical languages involved (16), the proper use of textual criticism (17), the study of the literal sense or "meaning intended by the author" (23-26), the use of history to uncover the circumstances in which books and passages were written (31-40), and the employment of literary analysis effected according to literary genres and of form criticism (37). In an opposite direction to that taken by Leo XIII, Pius XII wished to defend the Scriptures from an overly spiritualized and dogmatic interpretation that might impugn or devalue the benefits of historical-critical analysis. In 1964 the PBC issued an instruction called *Sancta Mater Ecclesia* on the historical truth of the gospels, much of which is contained in Vatican II's *Dei Verbum*. It described the three stages by which the Gospel message had come down to us: from Palestine through the church to the gospel text. *Sancta Mater Ecclesia* approved the use of modern exegetical methods and even went so far as to defend exegetes from unfair criticism. While the spiritual and theological meanings of the sacred texts must not be neglected, the literal meaning was to be sought first.

The third or present period was inaugurated by the PBC document *The Interpretation of the Bible in the Church* (1993). This document marked the centenary of *Providentissimus Deus*. *The Interpretation of the Bible in the Church* summarized the church's late-twentieth-century understanding of the exegesis of Scripture. It attempted to take into account recent discoveries (e.g., the Dead Sea Scrolls) and surveyed certain new exegetical methodologies such as feminist and sociological analyses. It gave one of the strongest ever recommendations for using the historical-critical method. This latter it deemed to be

> the indispensable method for the scientific study of the meaning of ancient texts. Holy Scripture, inasmuch as it is the Word of God in human language, has been composed by human authors in all its various parts and in all the sources that lie behind them. Because of this, its proper understanding not only admits the use of this method but actually requires it. (*The Interpretation of the Bible in the Church* I. A. Introduction, 34)

However, *The Interpretation of the Bible in the Church* notably tried to relate the literal and spiritual meanings of the text and thus encouraged the reconciliation of modern with classical methods and their different emphases. Where initially Catholic scholarship had remained conservative with regard to the new methods, tending to use the acceptable elements and results of Protestant exegesis, later exegesis, especially in the 1970s and 1980s, had become thoroughly immersed in the new methods and avowedly ecumenical. Indeed, in recent years Catholics have often been the leading practitioners of biblical scholarship, as seen in the celebrated *Jerome Biblical Commentary* (originally published in 1968 but revised and reissued since), edited among others by such notables as Raymond E. Brown (d. 1998) and Joseph A. Fitzmyer (b. 1914). On the other hand, other Catholic biblical scholars such as Luke T. Johnson (cf. his 2002 *The Future of Catholic Biblical Scholarship*) have warned that the historical-critical methods have limits, especially when used alone. These methods tend to be hegemonic, relativizing other methods, and yet are not in themselves theologically neutral; they often pit Scripture against the church, liturgy, doctrine, and prayer, rarely taking into account the ecclesial nature of the Bible. In any case, why should so-called critical (i.e., Enlightenment) scholarship take ideological preference over pre-critical (i.e., classical) scholarship so that the latter is systematically eclipsed? The new methods have not led to any agreed reconstruction of origins; there are as many views of X or Y as there are scholars. Moreover, their concern is with origins and not with succeeding or even preceding interpretations, with the result that the earlier something is, the truer it is deemed. Johnson speaks of the exegete's concern with the acorn rather than the tree, the isolation of a text from its organic development within the later tradition.

The 1993 PBC document itself, therefore, recognizes that historical methods when taken alone are insufficient for interpreting Scripture. Their strength is also their weakness. The aim of establishing the meaning of a text within its original context is laudable, yet there is also a need to apply that text to the church today (p. 41). This is why, some argue, other methods must be used too, especially those that try to situate a text within the Bible as a whole and as a document of faith. Indeed, the question that remains is: What is the relationship between the historical-critical (scientific) and dogmatic (traditional-ecclesial) interpretation of a biblical text? These methodological issues will be revisited in chapter 4.

The Liturgical Movement

Another highly important renewal movement associated with the *Nouvelle Théologie*, and one that paved the way for Vatican II, was the liturgical movement. This was closely bound up with advances in patristic studies and the recovery of ancient liturgical source texts.

The Liturgical Movement is widely acknowledged to have begun in France at Solesmes Abbey in the nineteenth century with Prosper Guéranger (d. 1875). But it also made considerable headway in the early to mid-twentieth century in Germany, centered around the Benedictine monastery of Maria Laach, thanks to Romano Guardini's foundational *The Spirit of the Liturgy* (1918) and the writings of others such as Odo Cassell (d. 1948), Pius Parsch (d. 1954), and Joseph Jungmann (d. 1975). The theological-practical aim of these reforming spirits was to reexamine the sources of the Roman Rite and thereby to restore the liturgy, and especially the Eucharist, as the real, affective center of all ecclesial, devotional, and pastoral life. The Benedictines were at the forefront of these new developments, and many of the new ideas were reflected in Pius XII's encyclical *Mediator Dei* (1947). This latter encouraged the "full, active conscious participation" of the faithful in the liturgy. Pius XII also initiated the 1955 Holy Week reforms, permitted the dialogue Mass, in which the people made certain responses in the Mass along with the servers, and attempted to popularize plain chant. These changes met with moderate success, many parishes forming choirs and attempting to sing simple chant and polyphony. Pope John XXIII introduced further changes to the Roman Missal in 1962, and it was this edition that formed the subject of Benedict XVI's motu proprio *Summorum Pontificum* (2007).

The liturgical movement reached its peak in the new vision of Vatican II's 1963 Constitution on the Sacred Liturgy, *Sacrosanctum Concilium.* The practical changes that were to be brought about were entrusted to the Consilium for the Implementation of the Constitution on the Liturgy, which Paul VI placed under the direction of the controversial Annibale Bugnini (d. 1982), a liturgist from the Pontifical Lateran University and author of the posthumously published *The Reform of the Liturgy 1948–1975* (1983). The consilium developed new liturgical directives and these led to the promulgation in 1970 of a new edition of the Roman Missal, which was itself reissued with minor revisions in 1975 and 2002. The consilium also in time conducted the wholesale renewal and revision of all the other liturgical rites.

It must be added that the liturgical changes brought about by the consilium in the postconciliar period have become a cause of controversy within the church. The nature, extent, and direction of the liturgical reform have been challenged by a growing reactionary movement among liturgical scholars that seeks a "reform of the reform" and even the reversal of some of the new directives. Their aim is to recover elements deemed in danger of being lost, such as the use of the Latin language and Gregorian chant, or doctrinal aspects of the liturgy potentially obscured by the repositioning of the tabernacle or the reorientation of the altar. This counterreform can be seen in, for instance, the writings of Klaus Gamber (d. 1989) and Peter J. Elliott (b. 1943), Joseph Ratzinger's *The Spirit of the Liturgy* (2000), and Alcuin Reid's *The Organic Development of the Liturgy* (2004).

5. The "Event" of Vatican II

Undoubtedly, the key event for theology in the last hundred years has been the Second Vatican Council, the twenty-first ecumenical council of the church. Its effects continue to reverberate across all areas of ecclesial life. The council's four sessions were held from 1962 to 1965 and were attended by over two thousand bishops, plus Catholic and non-Catholic observers. Vatican II was announced by Pope John XXIII in 1959. He spoke of the need for an updating of the church's life and doctrinal formulations for the sake of ecumenism and for evangelizing the modern world. Initially, while some were enthusiastic about the opportunity for renewal the council would afford, others, including members of the Roman Curia, were lukewarm. Once the council was under way, its participants realized that Vatican II had not only a life of its own but also a much deeper historical and theological significance, authorizing the bishops to adopt a more radical purpose than originally anticipated. The council in effect espoused a two-way method: *ressourcement* (back to the sources) and *aggiornamento* (updating). It was called a pastoral council because its aim was not to formulate a new dogma in the face of a difficulty but to teach the Christian faith in a pastoral manner and to foster ecumenical and human unity. Vatican II issued sixteen documents: four constitutions (on the liturgy, the church, revelation, and the church in the modern world), nine decrees, and three declarations.

All the conciliar documents assimilated the new insights of twentieth-century theology. Indeed, the theological style of these documents is distinguished by an approach that is above all ecumenical, not polemical, intending critically to appropriate the insights of other viewpoints; biblical, not philosophical, openly adopting scriptural categories; personalist, not scholastic, preferring the language of human experience to that of metaphysics; historical, not static and deductive, with a real sense of relating the faith dynamically to current concerns and historical developments; and dialogical, not exclusivist, espousing a worldview that seeks to be inclusive by addressing all people of goodwill.

One of the key theological concerns of the council, arising from its ecumenical intention, was ecclesiology: What does it mean to be the church of Christ in the modern world? *Lumen Gentium* eschewed the former institutional view of the church in favor of the church seen as the pilgrim people of God. In more recent times this, too, has been overlaid by a newer focus on other models of ecclesiology present in the council documents, notably eucharistic ecclesiology. The sense of the church as a communion has raised many issues in the postconciliar period about the relationship between the local and the universal church as well as between the Roman Catholic Church and other Christian communities, particularly the Eastern Orthodox churches. Thus, for example, John Quinn (b. 1929), in his *The Reform of the Papacy* (1999), called for the decentralization of some aspects of ecclesiastical governance from Rome. Recently again the issue of the wider ecumenism of the interreligious dialogue, the relationship of the church to the other world religions, and their place in God's plan of salvation has come to the fore.

All the pre–Vatican II theological renewal movements (biblical, patristic, liturgical) continued after Vatican II. Freed from neoscholasticism, anti-modernism, and out-of-date methodologies, Catholic theology then entered on a period of enormous vitality and creativity. A welter of innovative theologies emerged, including liberation theology, black theology, feminism, ecological theology, theology of religions, and inter-religious dialogue. Catholic theology in general became much more ecumenical in tone. At the same time, the "event" of the council, which for several years in the 1960s dominated the church's consciousness and caused many pastoral and planning decisions to be suspended, created a sharp sense of a before and an after, such that the period after the council was usually referred to as postconciliar. In the excitement of the day it was not uncommon for popular speakers to suggest that the church had been reinvented at Vatican II; a new era had opened up, with a "return to the sources" that made the postconciliar church much more similar to the early church than the degenerate clericalism and pedantry of the intervening centuries. On the other hand, in the less optimistic atmosphere of the early twenty-first century new historical studies have begun to emerge that take a more critical and detached view of the council, reviewing its negative as well as its positive aspects while assessing its genuine achievements and abiding historical significance.

The postconciliar period that the church continues to be passing through even in the early twenty-first century is marked by such features as the decline of scholasticism, pluralism, polarization, and an increasing presence of the magisterium. These will be considered in turn.

The decline of scholasticism-Thomism in favor of a wide variety of philosophies and approaches has already been referred to. Significantly, in a direction typical of the era, Pope John Paul II attempted a synthesis between Aristotelian Thomism and phenomenology, whereas Pope Bene-dict XVI, while especially influenced by Augustinian thought, has ad-opted a more scriptural and patristic style.

A second feature of the postconciliar period is its diversification and pluralism. Since Vatican II there has been a widening distinction between the style of theology done in universities and that done in monastic and seminary contexts. The former, founded largely on historical-critical methods of scriptural and general scholarship, has become increasingly issue-oriented, while the latter, oriented to the needs of pastoral and ministerial formation, continued by and large to follow the route mapped out by preconciliar patterns of formation. Far more laypersons study theology nowadays than clergy and religious. This has meant that Catholic theology has, on the whole, become much more academic and professional, in some cases remote from ecclesial life, practice, faith, and devotion, yet highly competent.

Postconciliar Catholic theology has been dominated by two giants, occasionally perceived to be in mutual opposition. The most significant—and one given a widespread reception in Protestant and Reformed circles too—was the German Jesuit Karl Rahner. Rahner was born in Freiburg in 1904 and studied under Martin Heidegger before completing his doctorate at Innsbruck, where after the war he taught dogmatics. He was a very influential *peritus* at Vatican II, and then succeeded Romano Guardini at Munich in 1965 before becoming professor of dogmatic theology at Münster, a position he held until his retirement in 1971. Toward the end of his life he became pessimistic about the prospects of the church, especially under Pope John Paul II, fearing that the optimism of the time of the council had yielded to reaction and authoritarianism. Rahner's theology was characterized by an attempt to update scholastic philosophy by bringing it into a critical encounter with the thought of Martin Heidegger. Thus in *Theological Investigations*, a multivolume collection of essays produced during his lifetime, and in his *Foundations of Christian Faith* (1978) Rahner attempted to reinterpret Aquinas and the classical tradition in existentialist and historicist categories. "The Trinity" was one of his most important essays; in it he posited that the "economic" and "immanent" Trinity were identical, God communicating himself to humanity as he really is in his divine life. Rahner also radically revised the scholastic theology of grace. He maintained that all human beings had a latent or unthematic awareness of God, which was the basic condition-of-possibility of their knowledge and freedom. By virtue of the death and resurrection of Christ, God offers salvific grace to all (the "supernatural existential"), even to non-Christians, so that they might come in some way to know the truth and exercise their freedom for good. This led to his celebrated theory that all who respond to such grace are "anonymous Christians."

Already in his life, particularly during the 1970s, and also since his death, Rahner has continued to command an immense following. Included in a long line of Rahnerian experts and scholars would be Herbert Vorgrimler (b. 1929), one of Rahner's students; Heinrich Fries (d. 1998);

Karl Neufeld, SJ, who wrote a critical biography of Rahner and his brother Hugo (d. 1968); Gerald McCool (d. 2005), author of several introductory works on neoscholasticism and the acclaimed *A Rahner Reader* (1975); and Mary Hines (b. 1943), coeditor of the *Cambridge Companion to Karl Rahner* (2005). A new generation has followed, some of whom are not uncritical, such as John O'Donnell (b. 1943), also an expert on von Balthasar; Karen Kilby (b. 1964), who has penned what is probably the most accessible of all introductory works, *Karl Rahner: A Brief Introduction* (2007); and Patrick Burke (b. 1964), whose *Reinterpreting Rahner* (2002) critiques central aspects of Rahner's philosophy.

If Rahner was the most widely read theologian of the 1970s and 1980s, the most widely read thinker since the 1990s has been Hans Urs von Balthasar, who besides being a theologian was also an outstanding musician and litterateur. Indeed, he completed a doctorate in German literature. Von Balthasar, born in Luzern, Switzerland, in 1905, initially joined the Jesuits. He studied under Erich Przywara (d. 1972), who was interested in the thought of John Henry Newman and pioneered new ways of reading Aquinas in relation to the phenomenology of Max Scheler and Edmund Husserl. Przywara introduced von Balthasar to the writings of de Lubac and inspired in him a lifelong interest in Scripture and the Fathers of the church. He thus came to reject the standard Thomistic fare in favor of an alternative canon that included the Platonizing tradition of Augustine and Bonaventure, the mysticism of John of the Cross, non-Catholic thought—notably that of Karl Barth, with whom he became close friends in the 1950s, and the Russian theologian Vladimir Soloviev—and the poetry of Gerard Manley Hopkins and others. Balthasar famously received into the church Adrienne von Speyr (d. 1967), a doctor, married woman, and mystic, who dictated to him her spiritual visions, which run to almost sixty volumes.

Von Balthasar's thought adopts the strongly christocentric focus of Karl Barth. In an opposite trajectory to Rahner he downplays the traditional scholastic emphasis on truth in favor of art, beauty, and poetry. He brings out the nuptial nature of Catholic thought (its "both-and" characteristic), as seen arguably in sexual complementarity, the Marian and Petrine dimensions of the church, and the inner life of the Trinity. Von Balthasar is best known for his sixteen-volume systematics (his trilogy), a sort of Catholic counterpart to Barth's *Church Dogmatics*. It is divided into three parts: *The Glory of the Lord*, a seven-volume work on theological aesthetics; *Theo-Drama: Theological Dramatic Theory*, a five-volume work on "theodramatics," that is, the action of God and the human response as shown above all in the events of Good Friday, Holy Saturday, and Easter Sunday; and the four volumes of *Theo-Logic*, principally about Christology. In the period after Vatican II, von Balthasar wrote in support of *Humanae Vitae*, increasingly contested the dominance of aspects of Rahner's theology of grace, and cofounded the theological journal *Communio*.

Like Rahner, von Balthasar too has developed a considerable following. Mention could be made of the prolific Dominican Aidan Nichols (b. 1948); the convert clergyman John Saward (b. 1947), author of *The Mysteries of March* (1990); David Schindler, dean of the John Paul II Institute in Washington, D.C., and an editor of *Communio*; Francesca Murphy (b. 1960), author of *Christ the Form of Beauty* (1995); and Dermot Power (b. 1952), who explored some of the pastoral implications of von Balthasar's thought in his *A Spiritual Theology of the Priesthood* (1998).

A third feature of the postconciliar era is the bewildering experience, for many, of theological polarization. This often focuses on the liturgy, issues to do with church governance, and matters relating to sexual and family morality. Vatican II coincided with an era of explosive historical, social, and technological upheaval, an upheaval still going forward, and its twin projects of *ressourcement* and *aggiornamento* quickly became embroiled in a volatile cultural context. This has resulted in reactive movements within the church for and against the council itself, with a struggle between classicizing and modernizing tendencies. The new academic theologians, mainly laity rather than priests or religious, often have a less intense or strict commitment to the church and its doctrinal positions, contesting especially ecclesiastical authority and traditional teaching on sexuality, ministry, and the role of women. They see the theologian's task less as one of explaining and defending magisterial teaching and more as rationally and meaningfully interpreting faith and revelation. In the 1970s and 1980s there was a growing chorus of dissent in moral theology, with an element of conflict between theology and the magisterium. This led the CDF in 1990 to issue an *Instruction on the Ecclesial Vocation of the Theologian*, dealing with dissent and also detailing the status of magisterial teaching and the various responses due to it. In the process a number of theologians fell afoul of church authorities, with the CDF issuing "Notifications" that condemned aspects of their thought.

One of two theologians who have been principal focal points for disaffected Catholics in the postconciliar period is Edward Schillebeeckx. He was "delated" to Rome for his *Jesus: An Experiment in Christology* (1979) and his later, twice reissued *Ministry* (1985). The former book was famously investigated by a CDF commission comprised of the Louvain biblical scholar Albert Descamps (d. 1980), one-time secretary of the Pontifical Biblical Commission; a Dominican scholar from the Angelicum, Albert Patfoort; and a Belgian Jesuit from the Pontifical Gregorian University, Jean Galot.

The other theologian is Hans Küng, the Swiss diocesan priest. Küng earned his doctorate at Paris, writing on the theology of Karl Barth, and was supervised by Louis Bouyer (d. 2004), a writer on spirituality and church history, one-time member of the International Theological Commission, and cofounder of the journal *Communio*. In the 1960s and 1970s Küng published a number of best-selling books, such as *The Church* (1967) and *On Being a Christian* (1974), and became arguably the leading progressive thinker of the time, certainly the best known. He challenged Pope Paul VI's reaffirmation of celibacy and the teaching of *Humanae Vitae*. Later he protested against John Paul II's supposedly authoritarian style and sparred with the then-prefect of the CDF, Cardinal Ratzinger. More recently, though, he has turned his attention away from church politics to interreligious dialogue, globalization, and the relationship between science and religion, and these formed the basis of private discussions, allegedly friendly and conciliatory, between himself and Benedict XVI at Castel Gandolfo in 2005. However, it was for his *Infallible? An Inquiry* (1970) that he was officially delated. In that book he proposed adopting the perhaps looser concept of "indefectibility" as a replacement for infallibility and eventually in 1979, after much controversy, his canonical mission to teach was withdrawn.

Other theologians censured by the CDF have included Leonardo Boff (b. 1938), for his *Church, Charism, and Power: Liberation Theology and the Institutional Church* (1981), which applied a Marxist dialectic to the structures of the church; Tissa Balasuriya for his *Mary and Human Liberation* (1990), which was said to deny the divinity of Christ and the doctrine of original sin; Anthony de Mello (d. 1987) for alleged assertions in his writings about the unknowability and cosmic impersonality of God and Jesus as one master alongside others; Matthew Fox (b. 1940), an exponent of so-called creation spirituality, for his *Original Blessing* (1983) and *The Coming of the Cosmic Christ* (1988); Roger Haight for his *Jesus, Symbol of God* (1999), in which he seemed to separate traditional Christology from Greek philosophical concepts; Jacques Dupuis (d. 2005) for his *Toward a Theology of Christian Pluralism* (1999), which appeared to relativize the universal salvific mediation of Christ and the mediatorial role of the church; and Paul Collins (b. 1940) for his *Papal Power* (1997), which was said to deny that the church of Christ is identified with the Roman Catholic Church.

On the other hand, potential polarization has spawned an increased interest in matters to do with theological method and the desire to maintain unity amid diversity. This was the supposedly positive focus of the 1990 CDF *Instruction on the Ecclesial Vocation of the Theologian*. Moreover, in theological circles the production of dictionaries and encyclopedias, and a new concern with foundations, has become evident, together with an outward thrust toward evangelization. This last can be seen in the emergence and spread of the new ecclesial movements.

Fourth, the postconciliar period has been marked by an increasing volume of magisterial pronouncements, particularly during the long pontificate of John Paul II (1978–2005). This was largely because of the ongoing implementation of the directives of the council. It was also in part a response to rapid social changes and advances in knowledge, which raised new questions or posed new problems, and in part a response to the challenges to the tradition posed by new philosophical and theological currents. The result was a run of important magisterial teaching and documentation, including the popular *Catechism of the Catholic Church* (1992, revised in 1997), the papal encyclicals of the 1990s on moral issues, and a series of important documents and clarifications from the CDF such as *Ad Tuendam Fidem* (1998) on the new oath of fidelity, *Dominus Jesus* (2000) on aspects of Christology and ecclesiology, *Collaboration of Men and Women in the Church and in the World* (2004) on the theology of being male and being female, and *Responses to Some Questions Regarding Certain Aspects of the Doctrine on the Church* (2007).

6. Liberation Theologies

One of the most important theological developments in the postconciliar period, if not in the twentieth century as a whole, was the emergence of liberation theology.

The Origins and Purpose of Liberation Theology

Today's various theologies of liberation emerged from the turbulent situation of Latin America in the late 1960s and the "irruption of the poor" (Gustavo Gutiérrez, b. 1928): i.e., the growing and disturbing awareness in North America and Europe of the violence, poverty, injustice, and oppression suffered by many in the developing world, and especially in Latin America. Theologians thus adopted an approach to theology that intended to begin from the real-life situation of people on the ground in order to interpret their situation in the light of the Gospel and lead to praxis or transformative social action (theology "from below"). To assist them with this they turned to the insights of social, economic, and political theories in order to develop a critique of the various structures and systems that were oppressive and from which the poor needed liberating, as well as to propose new ways of structuring the social order in the light of faith. Liberation theology is thus a prime instance of a theology that is interdisciplinary, looking beyond philosophy and entering into conversation with a wide range of disciplines.

In the Latin America of the 1960s, three factors (remote, general, and immediate) came together to form the matrix for liberation theology.

The first factor came from the remote context. This was the general evolution of Catholicism in the twentieth century, including the development of a comprehensive body of magisterial social teaching, the theological renewal associated with Vatican II, particularly the biblical renewal, and a general concern with the practical relevance of the Gospel along the lines marked out by the Pastoral Constitution on the Church in the Modern World, *Gaudium et Spes*.

The second factor derived from the general context of the Latin American situation. Mention should be made of the establishment by Pius XII in 1955 of the Latin American Bishops Conference (CELAM), representing the twenty-two episcopates of Latin America and the Caribbean. CELAM was to be an episcopal forum for coordinating pastoral strategy. Its five General Assemblies have set unique directions for the church in Latin America.

CELAM I (1956), held in Rio de Janeiro, established the headquarters organization in Colombia, with agencies and departments for organizing the life, teaching, and pastoral strategies of the church on a continental level. CELAM II (1968), held in Medellín, Colombia, was the historic milestone, the assembly called to implement the directives of Vatican II in the Latin American context. Its primary axiom was the need to interpret the signs of the times and so it adopted a theological method that was not deductive but inductive. It began with an analysis of the dire situation of the peoples of the continent and then sought to discern God's will in the light of it. Thus the assembly saw the church's task as not only to proclaim the Gospel but also to strive for justice, liberation, and development. The church should be prepared, it urged, to take a prophetic stance in relation to governments and multinational corporations: denouncing abuses, encouraging grassroots organizations, and showing solidarity with the poor. Medellín implicitly endorsed the positions and much of the language typical of the then-nascent theologies of liberation.

CELAM III (1979), held in Puebla, Mexico, endorsed Medellín. Yet many dissenting voices were raised against the supposed excesses of liberation theology. This gathering especially critiqued open endorsement of Marxist analyses and called for the reinsertion of liberation concerns into the wider social teaching of the church. CELAM IV (1992), held in Santo Domingo, Dominican Republic, was opened in person by Pope John Paul II. It further consolidated earlier positions but took into account the 1984 and 1986 CDF instructions and the collapse of communism after 1989. CELAM V (2007) held in Aparecida, Brazil, was attended by Pope Benedict XVI. It focused on evangelization and the need for formation of the faithful for mission.

The third factor came from the immediate pastoral context: the formation within Latin American dioceses in the period after Vatican II of *communidades de base* or Base-Level Ecclesial Communities (BLECs). BLECs are small lay-led groups within a parish or diocese, perhaps under a catechist, whose aim is to live a communal lifestyle based on the Gospel, including social, economic, and political functions. BLECs are a unique and highly significant feature of Latin American ecclesiastical life; there are said to be over one hundred and fifty thousand of them today, eighty thousand in Brazil alone. They were established as a reaction to the huge size of many Latin American parishes and the chronic shortage of priests and usually comprise about twenty families each, based in villages or *favelas*, the shantytowns on the margins of cities. The BLECs have a spiritual focus, gathering for daily prayer, Bible reading, and Holy Communion. They also have a social, self-help function, providing members with mutual support. Examples of the latter might include literacy programs, basic health care provision, farming cooperatives, and human rights initiatives. BLECs explicitly aim at relating Christian faith to daily life and so look for practical, transformative action. This is why they have always been the key addressee of the theologies of liberation, their central focus and chief concern. Indeed, liberation theology was written primarily, although not exclusively, for BLECs. Unsurprisingly, the BLECs have on occasion been targeted by political authorities when they have been perceived as a cause of unwelcome political activism and agitation.

Liberation theology is an activist and practical form of theology, a "feet-on-the ground theology," theology "from the underside of history," in the words of Gustavo Gutiérrez. It takes as its first principle the liberation of the oppressed from injustice, poverty, and all harmful political, economic, and social structures and conditions. It aims to reread the Christian faith in a new key, with a new way of understanding the church and its evangelizing mission in the world. The church is seen as existing not for itself but for others: its mission is to proclaim and effect the kingdom of God in history. To do this, it is said, the church must take the side of the poor: indeed, it must become in itself the church of the poor, the church of the people. Liberation theology thus attempts to interpret the misery and poverty endured by the majority of the world's South in the light of the Gospel in order to bring about transformative praxis. Consequently, it sees itself as a reaction against academic theology. To adapt the phrase Karl Marx took from Ludwig Feuerbach (d. 1872) about philosophy, theology is not about interpreting the world but changing it—actions, not propositions. The first protagonists included Gustavo Gutiérrez, a Peruvian priest sometimes called the father of liberation theology, author of the now-classic *A Theology of Liberation* (1972); Juan Luis Segundo (d. 1996), a Jesuit from Uruguay who wrote the influential *The Liberation of Theology* (1977); the Brazilian former Franciscan Leonardo Boff (b. 1938); his brother Clodovis Boff; and Jon Sobrino (b. 1938).

Liberation theology is characterized by four main themes or principles: a preferential option for the poor, a rereading and practical application of Scripture, the precedence of praxis, and the practice of ideological critique.

First, a preferential option for the poor: The Scriptures and tradition are reread to discern God's preferential (though not exclusive) action in history for the poor. God reveals himself through the poor. The aim is to stimulate the poor themselves to take on the revolutionary impulse of the Gospel ("conscientization"), through reforming the church itself to become poor (evangelical poverty) while showing solidarity with the poor, serving them, and struggling alongside them, even, if necessary, opting to support one social class over and against another. Much liberation theology attacks clerical lifestyles, calling for reform and conversion. The term "poor" here depends on the type of liberation envisaged. It can mean those oppressed not only by material poverty but also those suffering from sexism, racism, classism, colonialism, and other forms of cultural domination. On the other hand, the term "option" has been debated, since it might suggest that Christianity is chiefly about moral imperatives to the exclusion of the other redemptive aspects of the Gospel. This is why some speak of a preferential "love" for the poor. For instance, in *Sollicitudo Rei Socialis* (1987) John Paul II spoke of a "love of preference for the poor" that can inspire radical decisions (42).

Second, the preferential option for the poor is accompanied by a new reading of Scripture and a new practical application of it. Liberation theology focuses on the prophetic denunciations of Amos, the Israelite experience of the Exodus, Jesus' work among social outcasts, and the political dimensions of Jesus' death. For liberation theologians Scripture reveals how God acts in history on behalf of the poor. Jesus' suffering for justice was the cost of discipleship and his death was "the historical outcome of the kind of life he lived" (Jon Sobrino). Jesus' teaching was not about truth claims but about changing attitudes and behavior. Often liberation theologies use new or modern historical-critical methods of exegesis that start from the biblical text itself rather than from traditional dogmatic statements.

Third, liberation theologies insist that action or praxis precedes theology. This is the methodological starting point for liberation theology. We see and join God working in history to liberate the poor; then we go to the Scriptures to understand or interpret what we see. Liberation theology rejects the classical understanding of theology as wisdom or rational knowledge (*fides quaerens intellectum*) in favor of *fides quaerens actionem* or critical reflection on praxis (Sobrino). Theology is the second step (Segundo), "arising at sundown," that reflects on "praxis," a concept borrowed from Marxism to signify the specific struggle and action of human beings in history for social transformation. Many liberation theologians initially borrowed sociological and political analyses from Marxism. Thus Gutiérrez in *A Theology of Liberation* cited with approval a statement of Jean-Paul Sartre that as a framework for thought "Marxism cannot be superseded" (9).

Fourth, central to the method is ideological critique. Liberation theologies are all about taking a prophetic stance; the first aim is to unmask ideologies of privilege and unjust structures, even including those within the church. This is why liberation theologians have been highly critical of classical Catholicism and Euro-American theologies, and also of the original colonization and missionary endeavors within Latin America. In this regard attention is given not only to the individual and social dimensions of the Gospel but also to the societal or structural dimension, especially to critiquing those structures within the national and international community that cause poverty and injustice.

As a genre, liberation theology has evolved through three phases: 1968–84, 1984–89, and 1989 to the present. The first period, from 1968 to 1984, was the period of initial development from the 1968 CELAM II (Medellín) conference to the publication of the first CDF instruction in 1984. Then, from 1984 to 1989 came the middle revisionist period, from the publication of the two CDF instructions to the demise of communism in 1989. The years from 1989 to the present form another period. At present, liberation theology has become highly localized. There are different forms for Latin America, Asia, and South Africa, with attempts to write liberation theologies for Europe and North America. It has also become highly diversified, with new focuses on urban poverty, black consciousness, and gay liberation. Perhaps the greatest instance of this, a study in itself, is the relation with feminist theology and now with ecological concern.

In the 1970s and early 1980s liberation theology was practiced by a relatively small number of theologians, significantly those who had been trained in Europe and notably at the University of Louvain (KUL). An important early influence had been the thought of Johannes Baptist Metz and the Lutheran and evangelical theologians Wolfhart Pannenberg (b. 1928) and Jürgen Moltmann (b. 1926). Yet, once underway, the ideas of liberation theology began to attract enormous attention. They were widely disseminated, not only causing controversy within the church but also threatening to become a major force within Latin American politics. Conservative ecclesiastics eschewed the severance of once-strong ties between church and state, while right-wing military dictatorships rejected the Marxist ideologies apparently infiltrating the church. There were also more critical voices that rejected the new theologies. They challenged the apparent fusion of the Gospel with Marxism, the latent reduction of the Gospel to a message of earthly transformation, the implicit opposition of liberation theology to traditional religiosity and piety, and the hermeneutical rereading of Scripture.

Perhaps the most serious theological objection of the opponents of liberation theology was the easy correlation of liberation with salvation, the kingdom of God as a future reality (heaven) and Utopia as a this-worldly transformed social order (earth). They argued that where Marxist dialectic envisaged progress as inevitable, the outcome of orthopraxis and class struggle, the notion of the kingdom of God was of a different order since it was God's gift, something that "inrupts" from without, at a time and place God alone determines (Acts 1:6-7). Moreover, earthly progress as envisaged by Marxism failed to take account of human inauthenticity, with the result that in many communist states the only means or mechanisms for guaranteeing compliance were totalitarian.

The Current Status of Liberation Theology

By the early 1980s, liberation theologies had become increasingly diversified and geographically disseminated, exported notably to South Africa and the Philippines. However, in the period 1984 to 1989 the course of liberation theology as a whole was significantly altered by two sets of factors, one internal, the other external.

The internal set of factors was the impact on theology of the two CDF instructions issued in response to the growing chorus of dissent and unease. The first, "Instruction on Certain Aspects of the Theology of Liberation" (*Libertatis Nuntius*), was issued in 1984. Of the two it was the shorter and more trenchant. Its first target was the allegedly uncritical assumption by theologians of insights from the social sciences, particularly Marxism, which it portrayed as atheistic, collectivist, and exclusively focused on historical praxis and political struggle. Any dialogue with social science, it said, must give priority to theology, since the truth it proclaims and interprets is derived not from human wisdom but from divine revelation (VII.10). Its second target was the allegedly uncritical assumption of rationalistic biblical hermeneutics by theologians, especially exegesis that drew a sharp distinction between the so-called Christ of faith and the Jesus of history, the latter seen as a sociopolitical revolutionary (VI.10). The key oppression from which people needed liberation, *Libertatis Nuntius* insisted, was not just structural and social evil, as seen in politico-economic poverty, inequality, and injustice, but personal sin. Consequently, it added, there was an urgent need to proclaim Christ. Mission should not be pitted against the practical care of the poor and needy (VI.3), and the axiom "preferential option for the poor" should not be seen in an exclusivist sense, omitting the young, the wealthy, the aged, or other categories (VI.6).

The second CDF Instruction, *Libertatis Conscientia*, appeared in 1986. This longer document offered a much more positive appraisal of the theme of liberation. After an initial survey of the contemporary situation it explored sin as the root cause of human alienation in all its different dimensions and the theme of liberation as deeply rooted in the biblical tradition. Christians do have a mission in the world, it said, to critique injustice and to promote the values of the kingdom, the principles for which can be found in the church's social doctrine. Paragraph 60 discussed the relationship between temporal liberation and eschatological hope. Earthly progress, the instruction noted, must be carefully differentiated from the growth of the kingdom, for the two "do not belong to the same order." Nevertheless, it is thanks to the energy derived from the Christian life that human beings develop their temporal life, receiving the grace to overcome sinful and unjust situations.

Besides these internal factors, there was also an important external factor that changed the course of liberation theologies: the collapse of communism in the socialist states of Eastern Europe and the apparent triumph of a globalized neoliberal capitalism. As a consequence, despite neo-Marxist claims to the contrary, Marxism has evaporated, with an attendant loss of the dynamism created by political utopianism. Moreover, since the mid-1980s there has been extensive sociopolitical reconstruction within Latin America, with the ousting of military governments and the advent of democracy. Meanwhile, Pentecostalist and fundamentalist groups have made considerable headway, particularly in Brazil, causing an element of soul searching within Catholic circles, especially since these groups have not focused on the social aspects of the Gospel but on traditional piety and personal devotion to Christ.

These internal and external factors have had a profound impact on liberation theologies. Initially theologians were divided in their response to the points raised by the CDF instructions. There was considerable hostility. Leonardo Boff, for instance, eventually left the Roman Catholic Church, whereas Gutiérrez and others cautiously appropriated the new parameters laid down by the CDF and emergent in the then-current magisterium of John Paul II. Of course, not all liberation theology assumed Marxist analyses. Black theology always rejected Marxist analysis since as a genre it emerged not in Latin America but within a Western pluralist society. Again, Asian liberation theology, typified by the writings of the Sri Lankan Jesuit Aloysius Pieris in his *An Asian Theology of Liberation* (1988), also rejected the political liberation theme in favor of a social and religious liberation based on spirituality. More recently Gutiérrez and others have come to acknowledge the need for sociological dialogue partners other than Marxism, while viewing the South American continent's traditional religiosity and devotions more favorably. Indeed, piety or devotion need not be viewed as an opium, à la Marx, but as a distinctive cultural offering to the universal church as well as a motive power that can be harnessed for social change.

One of the central critiques of the 1984 CDF instructions was that the concerns of liberation theologies needed to be brought into a closer harmony with the general direction of church social teaching. To some extent it could be said that John Paul II made this project his own. His magisterium not only richly enhanced official social teaching but also mapped out a comprehensive anthropology able to ground the concerns of liberation theology while offering a bold critique and prophetic denunciation of regimes that impugned human rights and dignity. This project may be discerned in the three social encyclicals *Laborem Exercens* (1981), *Sollicitudo Rei Socialis* (1987), and *Centesimus Annus* (1991). In them

John Paul II can be said to have nationalized liberation theology, revising it and making it the universal theology of the church. The church was now depicted as the international supporter of human dignity, campaigning for the inviolable worth of every person, particularly the poor and weak. John Paul's social teaching spoke of the need for a true solidarity expressed in right and just economic and political relationships while actively promoting authentic human living and culture (a "civilization of love" and a "culture of life"). All of this was rooted in a theological anthropology with a christocentric focus: in the mystery of Christ is revealed the mystery of humanity. In *Veritatis Splendor* (1993) and *Evangelium Vitae* (1995) John Paul II declared that poverty and injustice, and everything making up the culture of death, were symptoms, not causes, derived from a loss of respect for the transcendent dimension of the human person. Once God is lost, so too is the human. Without God, humans become beings torn adrift, prey to dangerous ideologies of both the left and the right, and these cannot deliver the happiness and freedom they promise.

Today theologies of liberation continue to make a key contribution to the life and thought of the church, infusing old doctrines with new life. Their emphasis on praxis need not be essentially Marxist. After all, praxis had been espoused by many nineteenth- and twentieth-century theologians such as Maurice Blondel (d. 1949), Max Scheler (d. 1928), and Bernard Lonergan. Christian praxis was also the intention of the Cardijn Principle of "see-judge-act" that animated the spirituality of the Young Christian Workers (YCW) and the Catholic worker movements established by the Belgian Cardinal Joseph Cardijn (d. 1967). Furthermore, liberation theologies continue to offer a healthy critique of any establishment, sacred or secular, currently undergoing a spiral of decline, or any power center of inattention, silliness, unreasonableness, and irresponsibility.

A Note on Feminist Theologies

One particular derivative of liberation theology took form in the 1990s, namely, feminist theology. Feminism is a movement of thought and a campaign for sociopolitical action that runs across all domains of life, including the religious, but in its specifically theological form it has had an important impact on Jewish and Muslim as well as Christian theology. Its origins in the interwar years were in part Marxist, but it burgeoned in the 1960s in American white bourgeois circles. Christian feminism, as with other genres of liberation theology, is a theology from below and is based on the retrieval and interpretation of the specific experience of being a woman.

Feminist theologies have evolved in three overlapping phases: To 1980, 1980–1990, and 1990 to the present. The first period, up to 1980, was characterized by androgyny, as the Women's Liberation Movement sought to neutralize sexual difference in order to liberate women from the procreative function and enable them to take up the kinds of leadership roles within society at that time generally monopolized by men. This initial phase yielded in the 1980s to a more radically gynocentric or "womanist" form of feminism, in part a reaction to white middle-class androgynous feminism. Womanism emphasized women's experience, the distinctiveness and difference of being a woman, and the interaction of women with their cultural contexts and the call for liberation required in those contexts. Theologically this gave rise to regional theologies of women's liberation, as outlined by Virginia Fabella in her *With Passion and Compassion: Third World Women Doing Theology* (1988). However, since the early 1990s another phase of theological feminism has emerged, reflecting the growing concern with ecological issues ("ecofeminism"). Many of these theologies argue for a reversal of contemporary culture's androcentrism in favor of a more cosmocentric view of humanity that urges all humans to take greater responsibility for the natural environment and espouse sustainable lifestyles. Finally, mention should be made here of the emergence in this period of women's spirituality movements and Women-Church networks, often linked to peace and environmental awareness groups and sometimes to new forms of community living.

Mary Daly has oft been regarded as the foster mother of theological feminism. A former religious now avowedly post-Christian, she expressed in her first book, *The Church and the Second Sex* (1968), a bitter disappointment with Vatican II for saying almost nothing on the role of women. The church, she argued, was systemically misogynist, as seen for instance in Augustine's theology of original sin with its antifeminist portrayal of Eve. Her later *Beyond God the Father: Toward a Philosophy of Women's Liberation* (1973) called for a radical "depatriarchalization" (the deconstruction of male bias) of all the core symbols of Christianity. Depicting God as a father (male) and Christ as a son (male), with Mary (woman) subordinate to Christ (man), rendered Christianity irredeemably sexist and biased, its fixation with Father/Son love a pure idolatry. If God is male, Daly averred, then the male is God (19). Patriarchalism is the rape of life, and in this way Christianity pursues rape as a way of life. We need therefore to "castrate this system that castrates" and rid Christianity of its male

God, a project she calls "deicide." Her later books, such as *Gyn/Ecology: The Metaethics of Radical Feminism* (1978), in which the term God was replaced with Goddess and the "masculine" symbol of the cross with the "feminine" symbol of the tree of life, and *Pure Lust* (1984) developed further an anti-Christian sentiment: "We do not wish to be redeemed by a god, adopted as sons, or have the spirit of god artificially injected into our hearts crying 'father'" (*Gyn/Ecology: The Metaethics of Radical Feminism*, 9). More recently Daly, who regards herself as a post-Christian feminist, has devoted herself to the depatriarchalization of language.

Theological feminism is underpinned by particular philosophical positions, approaches, and methods. Central to this is gender analysis. Gender analysis is an ideological analysis of the church's Scriptures, traditions, theologies, liturgies, and power structures in order to identify the oppression of women in the history of the church, to recover the experience of women, and to critique and where necessary reconstruct the church's tradition. Its aim is to transform the church into a global movement for women's (and men's) liberation. Rosemary Radford Ruether (b. 1936), a key practitioner, in her *Women and Redemption* (1998) identified the two theologians from the Catholic tradition whom many women have found most objectionable, namely, Augustine and Aquinas. Augustine, after his own inner struggle with temptation, is said to have portrayed women in a negative light, correlating maleness with mind and reason and femaleness with the body and the passions. Aquinas, in taking over the philosophy of Aristotle, a philosophy unable metaphysically to account for gender, allegedly believed that God created woman principally for the purpose of procreation:

> I answer that it was necessary for woman to be made, as the scripture says, as a "helper" to man; not, indeed, as a helpmate in other works, as some say, since man can be more efficiently helped by another man in other works, but as a helper in the work of generation. (ST I-I, q. 92, a. 1)

Moreover, Aquinas is said to have stated elsewhere that women were naturally subject to men because they are the weaker sex, men having greater intellects (cf. ST I-I, a. 92, q. 1 ad 1 and 3).

Feminist theological scholarship is particularly active today, first, in biblical studies, where exegesis has attempted to reexamine and reinterpret the historical context and structures of the early church. Some scholars have proposed that the first Christian communities were essentially egalitarian and included female apostles and leaders, such as Junia and

Phoebe, but in subsequent generations the church, for pragmatic reasons, wrote these women leaders out of its memory and became progressively more patriarchal. Elisabeth Schüssler Fiorenza (b. 1938), in her *In Memory of Her: A Feminist Theological Reconstruction of Christian Origins* (1983) and *Bread Not Stone: The Challenge of Feminist Biblical Interpretation* (1984), argues that the biblical evidence provides the basis for a "discipleship of equals," but she resists historicizing the data. Again, the Scripture scholar Sandra Schneiders in her *Beyond Patching: Faith and Feminism in the Catholic Church* (1991) and *The Revelatory Text: Interpreting the New Testament as Sacred Scripture* (1991) has explored the complex issues involved in feminist biblical hermeneutics. Another area of feminist scholarship is systematic theology. Thus Elizabeth Johnson (b. 1941), in her classic *She Who Is: The Mystery of God in Feminist Theological Discourse* (1992), discussed the father/mother aspects of "G*d" or "Gad" (terms used instead of God in order to remind the reader not to think patriarchally), while others such as Anne E. Carr (d. 2008) have discussed ecclesiological issues, particularly the use of inclusive language, the possibility of the ordination of women, and women's roles within the church. A third domain of feminist scholarship is moral theology, where gender analysis has concentrated on reproductive rights, social justice, liberation from patriarchy, and sustainability. Rosemary Radford Ruether, for example, in her *Gaia and God: An Ecofeminist Theology of Earth Healing* (1992), argued that the female sense of embodiment has helped all human beings to recognize their interrelatedness with the natural world, the cosmos, and the environment, and thus to adopt more ecologically sound lifestyles.

One issue currently in the foreground is the theological meaning and value of being male and being female: What is the purpose in God's plan of being male and being female? The quasi-metaphysical issue in the background here is whether humans are essentially androgynous, maleness and femaleness being a quality like the color of one's skin. Or are males and females like two incommensurable species? Some feminist theologians have adopted monist (androgynous) anthropologies whereas others, such as Uta Ranke-Heinemann (b. 1927) in her *Eunuchs for the Kingdom of Heaven: Women, Sexuality, and the Catholic Church* (1990) and Catherine Mowry LaCugna (d. 1997), author of *Freeing Theology: The Essentials of Theology in Feminist Perspective* (1993), adopt dualist anthropologies. Still others, such as Lisa Sowle Cahill (b. 1942) in her *Sex, Gender, and Christian Ethics* (1996), Prudence Allen, and Joyce Little adopt complementarist anthropologies that variously view males and females as different yet ordered to one another. Recently, the magisterium seems to have lent support to this last position. John Paul II in his *Letter to Women* (1995), written for the UN Beijing conference on women, the *Catechism of the Catholic Church* 369–73, and the CDF *Letter to Bishops on the Collaboration of Men and Women in the Church and in the World* (2004) discussed the current state of the question and sought to establish an ontological basis for sexual difference, seeing men and women forming together a "relational uni-duality." Moreover, in the one hundred and twenty-nine papal audiences he gave from 1979–84 on the theology of the body, John Paul II asserted that the meaning of being male and female was God's call to be a procreative communion of persons, and that this communion of persons was an image on earth of the communion of the Blessed Trinity. These "nuptial" theologies are clearly influenced by the foundational work of Henri de Lubac and his retrieval of the thought of Origen.

Feminist concerns have been in the forefront of theology for several decades now. Indeed, theological feminism, as with liberation theology in general, is an interesting example of the development of doctrine from below. Feminism started within ecclesiastical domains, passed into the secular mainstream, then reentered the religious realm. The challenge was then taken up by theologians and finally by the magisterium.

7. Crises in Moral Theology

The current crisis in moral theology (one might well speak of crises, in the plural) has many aspects. It centers on family and sexual morality, extends to increasingly complex biomedical issues such as those relating to the beginning and end of life (e.g., reproductive technologies and palliative care), and more generally involves the notions of conscience, freedom, the sense of sin, and the ecclesial/sacramental mediation of forgiveness. It arose historically in the aftermath of Paul VI's encyclical letter *Humanae Vitae* (1968).

The history of this encyclical and its reception is a study in itself. Coming as it did in the midst of the social and sexual revolutions happening in many Western societies in the 1960s—and given that a majority of Catholics, including those on the original commission set up by John XXIII under the chairmanship of the French Jesuit and moral theologian Gustave Martelet, had wanted or at least were expecting a change in official teaching—*Humanae Vitae*, by reiterating the ban on artificial methods of contraception, sparked a crisis. The moral theology of Tridentine Catholicism had been heavily casuistic, the application of the general norms of the natural law and the commandments to specific cases of "What if?" There was little or no reflection on the actual foundations of morality. With hindsight it could be argued that official teaching, particularly on matters of sexual morality, was underdeveloped. Harsh or aberrant applications were frequently made in pastoral practice. The new theological movements leading to and from Vatican II, however, led moral theologians to seek a less scholastic and more biblical, christocentric basis for Catholic morality. They sought to transform the Tridentine "system" of merit and sin, reward and punishment, with new philosophies of human personalism based on God's infinite love and his desire for our happiness. Yet these new approaches tended to put less emphasis on individual actions and more on general intentions. The result was a conflict about moral absolutes between two groups, the deontologists and the teleologists.

On the one hand, the deontologists (Gk. δεων, "duty"), that is, theologians such as John Finnis, professor of law at University College, Oxford; William May, coauthor of *Catholic Sexual Ethics* (1998); Germaine Grisez; and the Dominican priest Benedict Ashley stressed or focused essentially on duty. They argued that actions were to be evaluated principally as right or wrong in themselves in the light of natural law. For example, does this or that action—say, using condoms—conform to the moral duty and norm?

On the other hand, the teleologists (Gk. τελοσ, "end") questioned the viability of the notion of natural law and instead stressed the consequences of actions. Thinkers such as the Redemptorist theologian Bernard Häring; the American Jesuit and popular religious writer Richard McCormick (d. 2000); Charles Curran (b. 1934); Joseph Fuchs (d. 2005), who chaired Paul XXIII's Papal Commission for the Study of the Problems of the Family, Population, and Birth Rate prior to *Humanae Vitae*; Louis Janssens from KUL (d. 2002); Franz Scholz (d. 1998); and the Liverpool priest Kevin Kelly (b. 1933) have argued that actions have to be evaluated principally by their intentions and consequences. There could possibly be certain circumstances in which the end might justify the means. For instance, condoms could be used as a last resort within a marital relationship if the husband had AIDS and they helped prevent the infection of the wife. What matters for teleologists is the person's fundamental option, her or his basic life choice and orientation toward good or evil in the light of which individual actions need to be interpreted.

The magisterium became embroiled in this conflict, perhaps most notoriously in the Charles Curran affair of 1986. Curran had first come to prominence in 1968 when he, along with a group of over six hundred Catholic theologians, issued a response to *Humanae Vitae*. Later he brought into question a number of the church's other teachings on moral issues, including premarital sex, masturbation, contraception, abortion, homosexual acts, divorce, euthanasia, and *in vitro* fertilization. Things came to a head in 1986 when the Vatican ordered Curran to be removed from the faculty of the Catholic University of America, although Curran continued to maintain a right to dissent from non-infallibly defined teachings.

John Paul II himself was a specialist in moral philosophy and anthropology. He is said to have developed a new way forward with his celebrated theology of the body and the recovery of a Trinitarian perspective on human relationality. These new lines of magisterial teaching have been taken up subsequently by a number of thinkers supportive of the teaching of *Humanae Vitae*, such as Janet Smith (b. 1950), author of *Humanae Vitae: A Generation Later* (1991). Moreover, while the encyclical letters *Veritatis Splendor* and *Evangelium Vitae* condemned proportionalism and consequentialism, they also, it is argued, established a new basis for moral theology in personalism, and in this way have mediated between the deontologists and the teleologists.

Chapter Three

Philosophy and Theology

In this chapter we look specifically at the influence of contemporary philosophies on recent Catholic theology. Some of the various philosophers and families of philosophy noted here have had only a general, oblique, or dispersed impact on theology, creating a direction, context, or concern against which a theologian does his or her theology. Others have had a more profound influence. Still others infringe upon important foundational areas of theology such as the philosophy of religion, fundamental theology, the language theologians use, their understanding of God, and the gender and liberation issues they wish to engage.

1. Which Philosophy for Theology?

Historically, theologians have used many different philosophies at different times, depending on what was current, available, or useful to the task at hand. Moreover, with the exception of the period when Leo XIII in *Aeterni Patris* (1879) imposed the use of scholastic philosophies, the magisterium of the church has never insisted on any one individual philosophy for use in theology.

In the New Testament era and during the first few centuries theologians seem to have used a plethora of philosophical ideas current in the Roman Empire of the time, above all the thought of Plato and, to a lesser extent, that of Aristotle. The New Testament contains elements of neo-Platonism and Stoic ethics, with their sharply defined notions of transcendence and self-sacrifice. Augustine was heavily influenced by the Middle Platonism of Plotinus. For several centuries in the early Middle Ages much of Aristotle's thought was "lost," but in the High Middle Ages, Aristotelian metaphysics were "rediscovered" and made available in translation. Aristotle offered a clear notion of the real, and this was put to use, most famously by Albert the Great and Thomas Aquinas. Scholastic thought in general saw philosophy as intimately connected with theology since it concerned logic, epistemology, and first principles, but Protestant theologians at the time of the Reformation generally rejected this medieval synthesis in favor of thought based exclusively on the principles of *sola fide* ("faith alone") and *sola scriptura* ("the Bible alone"). This has remained the Protestant orthodoxy ever since, although in the nineteenth century liberal thinkers took up anew the dialogue with philosophy, as is evident in the area of scriptural hermeneutics and the reception of traditional doctrine. Roman Catholic theology from the Council of Trent onward was largely wedded to the perennial philosophy, although later, at the time of the Enlightenment, some theologians explored the thought of Descartes, Leibniz, and Wolf, who discussed the natural sciences. From the Enlightenment onward, the discipline of philosophy and its concerns became much more sharply distinct from theology. After 1879, as noted, neoscholasticism became the norm within Roman Catholic theology until the mid-twentieth century. In the first half of the twentieth century theologians began to pay attention to post-Kantian thinkers, although usually in relation to Thomism. Since Vatican II the demise of neoscholasticism has opened the way for the adoption of a plurality of philosophies, even though Thomism still has a certain prestige.

What type of philosophy does a theologian require? How much philosophy does a theologian need? Indeed, as a theologian, why should one study philosophy?

The last question, the why of philosophy, is perhaps the most straightforward to answer. Bernard Lonergan's definition of theology, discussed earlier, is helpful. He envisaged theology as a mediation between a cultural matrix and the significance and role of a religion within that matrix. In other words, theology mediates between faith and culture. This helps us understand the purpose of philosophy for theology. Just as a religion needs a language, a culture, words, art, music, and symbolism to express itself, so too theology needs a philosophy as a "control of meaning" to clarify its concepts, methods, and questions, and to articulate and express those concepts, methods, and questions in terms meaningful to its culture. To mediate faith into contemporary culture in a manner that can be grasped by contemporary culture requires the translation of religious truths into forms readily accessible to that culture.

How much philosophy does a theologian need? Theologians first of all need to know enough philosophy to enable them to avoid a naïve and uncritical adoption of terminology, language, concepts, and positions that would ultimately undermine or subvert religion and be incapable of supporting the kind of truth claims they might wish to make. Philosophy discusses the nature of knowing, the nature of reality, the nature of value, and the nature of religion. Can humans ever know what is objectively true? How real are the things we know (e.g., the Real Presence)? Can what is truly good ever be known? Can the true religion ever be known? Theologians adopt philosophies in order to pursue and structure what might be a fruitful line of thought, one that might also stand up to challenge within a culture. Globally speaking, it could be said that philosophy provides theology with the "basic anthropological component," that is, with a systematic account of the human subject as the active recipient of God's gift of divine love in Jesus Christ. It provides an account of the human subject and recipient of divine revelation. Lonergan summarizes the philosophical task within theology in four specific questions:

THE PHILOSOPHICAL TASK WITHIN THEOLOGY	
Question for the Theologian	**Philosophical Requirement**
What am I doing when I am knowing? How do I know anything at all?	cognitional theory
Why is doing that "knowing"? What theories are there about knowing?	epistemology
What do I know when I know? Can I know the truth? Is my knowing "objective"?	metaphysics
Is it worthwhile? How can I know and do what is good and valuable?	ethics

Figure 6

If my philosophy can provide me, as a theologian, with a clear answer to each of these questions, then, Lonergan argues, I find myself equipped to mediate between religion and culture. In addition, it must also be acknowledged that the task of mediating between religion and culture requires theology to embrace other disciplines as dialogue partners besides philosophy, such as history, sociology, psychology, economics, politics, anthropology, and phenomenology of religion. This might suggest that philosophy has a reduced role nowadays. Yet many of these human sciences themselves lack clear foundations and a sense of integration, and so need to be philosophically grounded.

In the postconciliar period the role and prestige of philosophy within Catholic theology underwent something of a decline: By the 1980s, increasing fragmentation and pluralism in theology mirrored the same fragmentation and pluralism in philosophy. In many seminaries and Catholic universities, systematic philosophy had been downgraded and the traditional curriculum of two years' philosophy before three or four of theology, particularly for those in formation for the priesthood and religious life, had lapsed. To amend this situation, Pope John Paul II issued an encyclical letter on philosophy, *Fides et Ratio* (1998), which attempted to rehabilitate philosophy in Catholic circles and promote its use in theology, especially in seminaries and universities. The outcome of this remains to be seen.

Finally, what sort of philosophy does a theologian require? In the past theology borrowed from and expressed itself in many different types of philosophy. This is the case again today, both in theory and in practice. Could a theologian, therefore, select for use whichever philosophy he or she wants? Theoretically and in practice, the answer to this must be yes. However, the church's magisterium continues to recommend philosophy in the tradition of Thomas Aquinas and the classical tradition, although not necessarily in an exclusivist manner. In *Fides et Ratio*, John Paul II spoke of the "enduring originality of the thought of St. Thomas" (43-44) because of the harmony he saw between faith and reason and the manner in which he correlated them.

> This is why the Church has been justified in consistently proposing Saint Thomas as a master of thought and a model of the right way to do theology. . . . Profoundly convinced that "whatever its source, truth is of the Holy Spirit," Saint Thomas was impartial in his love of truth. He sought truth wherever it might be found and gave consummate demonstration of its universality. In him, the Church's Magisterium has seen and recognized the passion for truth; and, precisely because it stays consistently within the horizon of universal, objective and transcendent truth, his thought scales "heights unthinkable to human intelligence." Rightly, then, he may be called an "apostle of the truth." Looking unreservedly to truth, the realism

> of Thomas could recognize the objectivity of truth and produce not
> merely a philosophy of "what seems to be" but a philosophy of
> "what is." (John Paul II, *Fides et Ratio*, 44)

Leo XIII had found Thomism helpful as a sound and "realistic" philosophy for Catholic use. It clearly differentiated the natural from the supernatural and so was able to express the realities theology wished to discuss. It offered a comprehensive account of the *praeambula fidei* (preambles of faith) in its natural theology, such as the arguments for the existence of God and the nature of the human soul. As an amalgam of Augustinian and Thomist thought, classical philosophy was also to a certain extent "common sense" philosophy: that is, it appealed to everyday observation and to the "good sense" of its devotee. Interestingly, this was the philosophical approach of a number of Anglo-Irish writers, both Catholic and non-Catholic, of the nineteenth and early twentieth centuries, who, while not philosophers in their own right, nevertheless engaged in philosophical thought for the sake of their theological, apologetical, or literary output. Mention might be made of John Henry Newman (d. 1890), C. S. Lewis (d. 1963), G. K. Chesterton (d. 1936), Hilaire Belloc (d. 1953), Msgr. Ronald Knox (d. 1957), and J. R. R. Tolkien (d. 1973).

It has long been argued that an important characteristic of any philosophy used by Catholic theologians must be that, like Thomism and the classical tradition, it is "realistic," either in a common sense form or in the more nuanced form Lonergan terms "critical realism." Critical realism is the approach that is critically aware of its own epistemological and metaphysical presuppositions and is able to affirm, when the appropriate conditions have been fulfilled, that knowing can be objective and that reality and truth exist. Such features would meet the philosophical requirements relating to the relationship of faith and reason proposed by Vatican I and for which *Fides et Ratio* commended the philosophy of Aquinas. For John Paul II, contemporary philosophy had many blind alleys, not least because of the decline of metaphysics, which in turn had been caused by a loss of confidence in the ability of human reason itself. Any philosophical position adopted for use within Catholic theology must, he argued, acknowledge implicitly or explicitly that human knowing is possible and that the truth can be affirmed. A realistic epistemology is required by the need to affirm that doctrinal statements have a permanent validity, and a realistic metaphysics is required by the need to affirm that the truths being taught (e.g., the existence of God or the divinity of Christ) are actually true or real.

2. The Influence of Philosophies on Recent Catholic Theology

The philosophies used in Catholic theology today run largely within one of three streams: epistemological, metaphysical, and linguistic. The epistemological philosophies are concerned with the knowing subject. Since Kant's "turn to the subject" and his distinction between the noumenal and the phenomenal, the issue of whether humans can know anything objectively or for certain has become dominant, and these concerns are reflected in theologies. The metaphysical streams in philosophy are concerned with the object known, and the theologies that espouse these philosophies often show concern with doctrine. The linguistic philosophies, as their genre suggests, concentrate on language, the value of symbols, and the clarity of concepts, all of which are put at the service of theology. Interestingly, the distinct concerns of each stream—the epistemological, the metaphysical, and the linguistic—come to the surface in many contemporary theological and pastoral discussions. For instance, was religious education and catechesis in the past overly concerned with the contents of revelation (metaphysics) and insufficiently concerned with the language being used (linguistics) and with religious experience, personal conversion, and how people come to know God (epistemology)? And is much current religious education and catechesis overly concerned with method (epistemology) and the correct language (linguistics) and not enough with sound content (metaphysics)?

Here we will consider the philosophical families of personalism, phenomenology, and existentialism, Marxism and other sociopolitical movements of thought, analytical philosophies, historicism and process thought, hermeneutics, late-modernism/postmodernism, and Thomism. The order of treatment is somewhat random. Sometimes several philosophies overlap in the same theologian's work, or a place where theology is done is occupied by theologians with different philosophical approaches. At other times a school of theology develops that has broadly the same philosophical commitments. On the other hand, there are other philosophical influences latent in current (Catholic) theology that are not examined here, including those that make use of indigenous philosophies.

Personalism, Phenomenology, and Existentialism

These three strands of philosophical thought—often in reality attitudes or approaches more than fully worked out systems—are in origin, theory, and practice frequently intertwined. They reached their apogee in the mid-twentieth century, becoming widespread as much in popular culture as in academic circles. In their religious forms they were particularly influential on the theological trajectories leading to and flowing from the Second Vatican Council.

Personalism is a form of humanism, with wide-ranging social, economic, and political consequences, that affirms the absolute value of the human person as the only "real" being in the world. Its remote origins lie in the writings of Kant, who, although not himself a personalist, asserted that persons cannot be valued merely as a means to the ends of others but possess a dignity and an absolute inner worth of themselves. As a movement, however, personalism is usually traced to Borden Parker Bowne (d. 1910) at Boston University. Bowne had been taught in Germany by Rudolf Hermann Lotze (d. 1881), the teacher of Edmund Husserl. Personalism was taken up in the interwar period in France by Emmanuel Mounier (d. 1950), founder of the influential philosophical journal *Esprit*, and also significantly by the Thomist scholar Jacques Maritain (cf. his 1947 *The Person and the Common Good*). Maritain was one of the key figures who drafted the United Nations Universal Declaration of Human Rights in 1948 and an erstwhile defender of the democratic ideal. Both Mounier and Maritain inspired postwar American radicalism and notably Dorothy Day (d. 1980), founder of the Catholic Worker Movement. Personalism also had a wide-ranging impact on the fundamental ideals of the European Union and of the various European Christian Democratic movements. Yet perhaps strangely, apart from the writings of the Canadian social and political philosopher Charles Taylor (b. 1931), personalism seems to have been largely ignored in recent Anglo-American political philosophy.

Phenomenology (Gk. πηαινομενον, "what appears") is the study of "things as they are," their appearances, what presents itself in conscious experience, as the basis and means of an account of the ontology behind phenomena. Phenomenology thus takes the intuitive experience of phenomena as its starting point and tries to extract from it the essential features of experiences and the essence of what humans experience. It involves a systematic return to the "data of things in themselves" (*zu den Sachen*) while making an *epoché*, a bracket or a bracketing off, of metaphysical and theological presuppositions, in order to generalize the essential features of an experience. Edmund Husserl (d. 1938), a German Jew and convert to Christianity who was inspired by the thought of Franz Brentano (d. 1917), is usually credited with its twentieth-century development. Husserl paid particular attention to the study of the structures and activities of human consciousness such as thinking, feeling, valuing, and loving as experienced from the first-person point of view. For him the central structure of an experience is its intentionality, its being directed toward something else, as much as its being an experience of or about an object. He went on to distinguish the realms of common sense and theory and to develop the notion of horizon. Phenomenology as a discipline is distinct from, but closely related to, ontology, epistemology, logic, and ethics, and in recent philosophy of mind, key phenomenological issues such as intentionality, consciousness, *qualia*, and first-person perspective have come to the fore.

Closely related to both personalism and phenomenology is existentialism. Existentialism or "existential phenomenology" is concerned with the meaning of existence and what it is like to be human. Its origins go back to nineteenth-century thought, particularly that of Søren Kierkegaard and Friedrich Nietzsche (d. 1900), but existentialism became a popular movement in France and Germany during the early- to mid-twentieth century thanks to the novels, plays, radio shows, and films its proponents wrote or inspired. Much existentialist thought is infused with Nietzschean nihilism, the denial of the meaningfulness of human existence and morality. It deals with issues such as dread, boredom, alienation, the absurd, freedom, commitment, and nihilism. For Jean-Paul Sartre, humans are alienated and anguished in face of a world that is ultimately absurd; in his novel *Nausea* (1940) and the academic treatise *Being and Nothingness* (1943), he depicts the human being as "a useless passion." The Algerian-born novelist Albert Camus, killed in a road accident in 1960, takes a parallel view of being human in *The Myth of Sisyphus* (1942). In that work he developed his "philosophy of the absurd," also found in his *The Outsider* (1942), *The Plague* (1947), and *The Rebel* (1951). Similar positions were reflected in the German author Franz Kafka (d. 1924) in *The Castle* and *The Metamorphosis*. Another existentialist thinker of note was Sartre's lover and lifelong companion, Simone de Beauvoir (d. 1986). Besides an insightful autobiography, she wrote monographs on philosophy, politics, and social issues, particularly *The Second Sex* (1949), an analysis of the oppression of women, now a classic text for modern feminism. Not all existentialists, however, saw humans as alienated from the world. Some envisaged a possible reconciliation. The Jewish philosopher Martin Buber (d. 1965), in his *I and Thou* (1923), proposed that humans could achieve meaning and happiness, a reconciliation with existence, through love and relationship. Gabriel Marcel (d. 1973), one of the first existentialists—indeed, he is credited with having invented the term—offered a Christian version of existentialism in dialogue with neoscholasticism. The author of over thirty plays as well as *The Mystery of Being* (1951) and *Man Against Mass Society* (1955), Marcel argued that humans must struggle to protect their subjectivity from annihilation by modern materialism.

Mention should also be made here—although he is in a category of his own—of the truly original thinker Martin Heidegger (d. 1976), the star pupil and research assistant of Husserl. His famous *Being and Time* (1927) starts with the riveting question: "Why something rather than nothing?" Humans are the only beings in the world, he says, who can stand out from the world (*ek-stasis*) to ask this. What is more, humans do so with a sense of responsibility and concern (*Sorge*) and this can be the cause of dread (*Angst*). The greatest *Angst* for humans is death, and yet humans find themselves as beings oriented toward it. Death is the horizon to living, that which gives life its sense of urgency. Consequently, if authenticity is to be achieved, humans must reach a reconciliation with death.

Personalism, phenomenology, and existentialism as intertwined currents of thought have had an enormous impact on modern Catholic theology. More than any other philosophical stream they have helped to bring about a long-gestated paradigm shift as much in popular culture as in theology. They have acted as a conduit for Enlightenment modernity, with the result that today's culture is methodically anthropocentric. Where the medievals inhabited a unified worldview focused on God and eternity, modernity in its fragmentation is focused on life in this world. Consequently, recent theology has itself sought to take an anthropological turn, to begin from and concern itself with the relevance of Christian faith for human life in the here and now. This is especially evident, albeit in different ways, both in the magisterium of John Paul II, who helped draft some of the key sections of *Gaudium et Spes*, particularly paragraph 22, and Benedict XVI. The new approach crystallized in the theological anthropology of John Paul II's *Redemptor Hominis* (1979), in which theology's starting point was inverted. The encyclical began not with God but with the human, although in the writings of John Paul II this ascending or inductive trajectory from below was never effected without being informed by the descending or deductive trajectory of divine revelation from above. John Paul II, building on Henri Bergson and Jacques Maritain, stressed the theological foundation of the human person in the Trinity: the human person is thus always a person in community, but one called to take real, moral responsibility for his or her actions.

Personalism, phenomenology, and existentialism have infused theology with a new concern for meaning and relevance. Recent theology tends to take seriously "things as they are," to begin with the mystery of creation, to unpack the *pro nobis* ("for us") meaning of revelation—what revelation means for life and the world—as the Nicene Creed proclaims: *qui propter nos homines et propter nostram salutem descendit de caelis* ("who for us and for our salvation came down from heaven"). It explores not only the consequences of revelation for spirituality and belief, as in the classical, wisdom-rational tradition, but also its human and personal meaning.

On the other hand, in the immediate postconciliar period some theologians reacted against excessive personalism in favor of a more practical theology that sought to show how Christian discipleship was dynamically relevant to social, political, and economic issues. This led to the development of political theology, and more recently to concern with the way the earth's ecosystems are managed (eco-theology). In all these endeavors theology has been open to dialogue with disciplines other than philosophy in order to demonstrate how Christ can redeem humans from the multiple enslavements to which they have become prey.

In the Catholic theology of the immediate postconciliar period, existentialism and personalism offered alternative philosophical dialogue partners to Thomism. Their pervasive effect can be seen in much of the theology of the 1960s and 1970s, notably in the writings of Gabriel Moran (e.g., *Theology of Revelation* [1965]), the later Schillebeeckx, and René Latourelle (e.g., *Man and His Problems in the Light of Christ* [1983]). Theologians tried to express the meaning of traditional theology in terms of human experience, psychological fulfillment, and personal well-being. The language of personal experience also suffused magisterial documents, and unsurprisingly *Dei Verbum* (1965) chose Johannine language to introduce its tract. Other theologians, notably Karl Rahner, were entranced by Heidegger. Rahner, in fact, developed an existentialist reading of Aquinas in light of Heidegger. Mention should also be made once again of the highly influential Lutheran Scripture scholar Rudolf Bultmann, long a professor of New Testament at the University of Marburg. In his *Theology of the New Testament* (1953) Bultmann claimed that Heidegger had, all by himself, discovered the Gospel outlook on the human condition. In other words, for him Heidegger's existentialist analysis was a secularized, philosophical presentation of the New Testament view of being human. Human being is a being ever in the moment of decision between the past and future. When the Bible is read, the Word of God challenges the listener to make an existential choice: either to accept responsibility and live authentically or to lose herself or himself in the variety of outside pressures that try to deny freedom. For Bultmann this process was linked with "demythologization," the hermeneutical tool that seeks to reinterpret the Scriptures by freeing the message of the Bible from such first-century mythological and prescientific concepts as the three-story universe (heaven, earth, and underworld). Through demythologization the exegete can thus reexpress the essential Gospel message or *kerygma*, presenting it to the modern reader or listener as an existential challenge.

Personalism and phenomenology were important influences on the intellectual development of Karol Wojtyla, the future Pope John Paul II. As a student at the Angelicum, supervised by Garrigou-Lagrange, Wojtyla wrote on St. John of the Cross before heading to Lublin to study the phenomenology of Max Scheler under the eminent Roman Ingarden. From this, Wojtyla acquired an abiding interest in human moral agency, evident in his important philosophical work, *The Acting Person* (1969), which explores issues having to do with human life, nature, existence, the struggle to survive, human dignity, and freedom. The book was meant to be a "disentangling of the conflicting issues facing Man, which are crucial for Man's own clarification of his existence and the direction of his conduct" (4) and opposed the materialistic and positivistic tendencies of some modern philosophies. John Paul II's social and moral encyclicals remained firmly within the Catholic tradition of personal and social morality, yet his explanation of the origins of moral norms was largely drawn from a personalist perspective, albeit a personalism rooted theologically in the Trinity. His writings have subsequently influenced a generation of Catholic theologians who have developed a theology of the family and social order.

Phenomenology is a key methodological approach for the new religious sciences such as phenomenology of religion, comparative religion, and philosophy of religion, all of which methodically aspire to be faith neutral. The growth of "religious studies" is typical of this approach and is often associated with the Scotsman Ninian Smart (d. 2001), founder at Lancaster of one of the first university departments of religious studies. He identified what are arguably the seven universal dimensions of religious belief (experience, society, narrative, doctrine, ethics, ritual, and material). But more generally, phenomenology has had a considerable impact on the style and feel of theology: that is, rather than beginning from first principles, theologians often begin from a survey or study of how things are, the "start where they are" mentality. This can also be seen, as noted, in Vatican II, notably in *Gaudium et Spes*, and many more recent magisterial documents, which invariably begin with social and historical analyses. This is clearly a different route from those of the past.

Husserl had important philosophical followers such as Dietrich von Hildebrand and Emmanuel Levinas (d. 1995). He also had an important influence on theology. His disciples included Edith Stein (d. 1942), herself a converted Jew, who wrote about feminism (cf. *Essays on Woman*) and tried to bring phenomenology into dialogue with Aquinas. Stein studied empathy as the key to intersubjectivity and thus to epistemology (cf. *On the Problem of Empathy* [1918]), noting how all human knowing takes place in the context of personal relationships. Other pupils of Husserl included Maurice Merleau-Ponty (d. 1961), author of *Phenomenology of Perception* (1945), and also the prodigious Max Scheler (d. 1928), who developed a personalist account of being human in which religion played the key role in personal and interpersonal development. Scheler was a singular influence on the Lublin Thomist school and, as noted above, on John Paul II. Yet another of Husserl's students was Roman Ingarden (d. 1970), who wrote on the philosophy of the human person, free will, and responsibility. It was Ingarden who supervised Karol Wojtyla's doctorate on Scheler.

Another instance of the influence of personalism and phenomenology on Catholic theology can be seen in the Dutch eucharistic controversies of the late 1950s and early 1960s. At that time Dutch theologians, notably Piet Schoonenberg (d. 1999) and the early Edward Schillebeeckx, sought to find new ways of expressing and explaining the nature of the Eucharist and especially the eucharistic transformation. They sought to transcend the traditional language of substance and accidents. Concentrating on interpersonal relations, theologians envisaged the Eucharist as a communal meal. Meals are about much more than food and drink; they are social occasions that enhance human and social relationships. In the Eucharist, Jesus gives the bread and wine a new meaning (trans-signification) and a new purpose (trans-finalization), as effective symbols of his redemptive love. The elements are changed insofar as they acquire a new significance and a new finality, that is, they bring about union with Christ and union among the eucharistic participants. This is why, they argued, the terms trans-signification and trans-finalization were preferable to the traditional scholastic term "transubstantiation." However, other theologians rejected this on the grounds that the alternative terminology failed to say what (if anything) happens to the elements themselves. The dispute was adjudicated by Pope Paul VI in his encyclical letter *Mysterium Fidei* (1965), in which he asserted that although these terms conveyed aspects of the mystery, they did not express adequately the nature of the change that occurs in the eucharistic mystery. Indeed, the bread and wine are only able to take on a radically new significance and finality because they contain a new reality. In other words, the change of meaning and purpose depend on a prior ontological change, and the best term so far to express this, Paul VI asserted, was "transubstantiation."

Marxism and Sociopolitical Philosophies

Marxism emerged from the context of German idealism. Where G. W. F. Hegel (d. 1831) in the nineteenth century saw progress as the outcome of a dialectical struggle of ideas—popularly if crudely simplified in the notion of "thesis-antithesis-synthesis"—Ludwig Feuerbach (d. 1872) applied Hegel's dialectic to matter. He denied transcendence and deemed religion an anthropomorphic projection; religions were human needs writ large. Feuerbach's ideas were modified by Karl Marx (d. 1883). In his *Das Kapital* (first published in 1867 but later reedited by his friend and collaborator Friedrich Engels) he applied Feuerbach's theses to economics and politics. Marx argued that what motivates human dealings is material (financial) advancement. Historical progress is brought about by a class struggle for a classless and stateless society in which goods would be in abundance and in which all could share. Religion is like an opium because it takes away the seriousness of human efforts to live and work in this world. In a sense this Marxist-communist theory is the inverse image of modern individualist capitalism—the so-called Blue Marxism of the one-time British Prime Minister Margaret Thatcher—according to which material and economic advance is the key to individual happiness. In this latter, instead of collective planning, the choices of the individual consumer are paramount.

Twentieth-century theology found Marxism a profound challenge and continued to do so even after the collapse of the Berlin Wall in 1989. In the first half of the century Catholic theology took a negative view, focusing on the atheistic and totally anthropocentric bases on which Marxism was built. Theologians challenged the moral and social consequences of Marxism and the spectre of totalitarianism associated with those states that had adopted Marxist communism. Marxism attacked religion and in so doing reduced human dignity. Its emphasis on materialism at the expense of religion seemingly degraded the individual. In its vision of class struggle it did not take seriously the reality of sin, believing that progress would be inevitable and that totalitarian controls should be imposed to guarantee progress. But on the other hand some theologians, increasingly favorable to Marxism, sought to respond to the Marxist tenet (derived from Hegel) that the point of any philosophy is not to understand the world but to change it. After Vatican II many, keen to demonstrate the relevance of Christian faith to the state of the world, adopted an anthropological turn and developed the practical and political implications of the Gospel. As Johannes Baptist Metz once put it, since the Enlightenment faith had been privatized, something he saw reinforced by secularism, a view that "priests should remain in their sacristies." Today, however, theology must offer an incisive social, economic, and political comment.

As noted in chapter 2, the greatest influence of Marxism and Marxist analyses was on the birth of the various liberation and activist theologies of the late 1960s. At that time the Latin American situation had become desperate, and liberation theologians, whose voices were heard at Medellín in 1968, began to adopt and adapt some of the insights and analyses of Marxist sociology and economic theory, applying them to both society and the church. More recently Marxist analyses have influenced the various types of activist theology such as theological feminism.

Another pervasive influence of Marxist analysis on recent Catholic theology has been the portrayal of theological arguments in political terms, that is, as a dialectical power struggle between left-wing modernizers or progressives and right-wing conservatives or traditionalists. The outcome of such struggles is not determined by rational argument (truth) but by the imposition of the will of one party over the other (power). This is the manner, for example, in which many popular Catholic journals and ecclesiastical commentators interpreted the papacy of John Paul II and the election of his successor, Benedict XVI: see, for instance, Andrew Greeley's *The Making of the Pope* (2005) and John L. Allen's *The Rise of Benedict XVI: The Inside Story of How the Pope Was Elected and Where He Will Take the Catholic Church* (2005). Many other disputed theological questions are nowadays treated politically, at least in popular journalism, as a struggle between left and right. This applies especially to views on liturgy, sexual morality, and ecclesiology. It also applies in a loose way to a new if somewhat defensive breed of Catholic apologetics that has emerged since the 1990s in American circles. Founded on a philosophy of Scottish common-sense realism—"let's call a spade a spade"—this new apologetics seeks to portray Catholicism as attractive to anyone of common sense, but especially to those of right-wing, fundamentalist, and evangelical tendencies. Proponents gravitate variously around the writings and broadcasts of Karl Keating (b. 1950), founder of *Catholic Answers*; the former Presbyterian preacher Scott Hahn (b. 1957), author of *Rome Sweet Home: Our Journey to Catholicism* (1993); the prolific Peter Kreeft (b. 1938) from Boston College; and the Jesuit priest and broadcaster Mitch Pacwa (b. 1951), author of *Some Heard Thunder, Some Heard God: The Catholic Church and American Culture* (2005).

Finally, mention should be made of schools of thought that developed or modified Marxism such as the Frankfurt School and also other non-Marxist-influenced sociopolitical theological thought. We have already referred to the writings of Johannes Baptist Metz and Jürgen Moltmann in Germany, and below we will mention John Milbank in England. Strands of social and political theology have also been developed in America, extending and developing the project of John Courtney Murray (d. 1967). He had long sought to reconcile the Christian faith with the political reality of modern religious pluralism, religious freedom, and the American political order. The American reformed theologians Stanley Hauerwas (b. 1940) and John Cobb (b. 1925), author of *Process Theology as Political Theology* (1982) and *Sustaining the Common Good: A Christian Perspective on the Global Economy* (1996) come to mind. Others include the neoconservative Catholic thinkers Michael Novak (b. 1933), author of *The Spirit of Democratic Capitalism* (1982); George Weigel (b. 1951), who wrote *The Cube and The Cathedral* (2005), comparing the condition of Christianity in Europe and America; and the Lutheran convert Richard John Neuhaus (d. 2009), author of *The Naked Public Square: Religion and Democracy in America* (1984); all of whom are staunch defenders of democratic capitalism.

Psychology

Psychology, the study of the human mind, is both an academic and an applied discipline, concerning itself with a wide range of issues to do with human behavior, the biological aspects of consciousness, cognitive development, personality disorders, and social adaptation. It is not, of course, strictly a philosophy, but a human or social science, yet one that implies or requires certain basic philosophical commitments; hence its inclusion here. Moreover, it appears here because its impact on contemporary culture as well as on recent Catholic theology is inestimable. At the very least it has created a universally pervasive "hermeneutics of suspicion" that endows all human attitudes and actions with hidden meaning. More positively, it has become a fruitful dialogue partner for theology and in particular for pastoral theology and spirituality.

Wilhelm Wundt (d. 1920), who established a laboratory for the study of psychology at Leipzig University, is arguably the father of modern psychology. Another early practitioner was the American philosopher William James (d. 1910), whose foundational *The Principles of Psychology* (1890) laid the groundwork for many of the questions later psychologists would focus on. However, it is Sigmund Freud (d. 1939) who is credited with founding the first great school of psychology, psychoanalysis. Through analyzing his patients and their dreams he developed theories of the unconscious mind and its desires, of repression and the transference of sexual desire toward other objects. He popularized such notions as defense mechanisms, Freudian slips, and dream symbolism. For Freud, humans had two fundamental drives: toward death and equilibrium, and toward movement, life, and pleasure. His study of the latter, the libido, which he argued was driven by the subject's sexual appetites, led to his famous analysis of regressive neuroses. Freud saw the human psyche as composed of the ego, the superego, and the id, but as he explained in *The Future of an Illusion* (1927), religion was for him the chief cause of psychological fixations and neuroses.

Freud had a number of followers who developed and substantially modified his theories. Best known was Alfred Adler (d. 1937) who, inspired by the philosophy of Nietzsche, asserted the centrality of the drive for power. Adler's most famous concept was the inferiority complex, which relates to self-esteem and its negative compensations. He was one of the first psychologists to explore feminism, arguing that the power struggle between men and women, between masculinity and femininity, was critical for understanding human psychology. Adler had an enormous impact on the disciplines of counseling and psychotherapy and in turn influenced Viktor Frankl and Abraham Maslow.

Another disciple of Freud was the French structuralist philosopher Jacques-Marie-Émile Lacan (d. 1981), who was also a psychiatrist and a doctor. He advocated a return to the meaning of Freud, with a renewed study of the Freudian concepts of the unconscious, the castration complex, the ego, and the centrality of language to any psychoanalytic work.

On the other hand, Freud's theories were, and still are, highly contested. In reaction to the subjective and introspective nature of Freudian psychology and its focus on the recollection of childhood experiences, another approach, known as behaviorism or behavioral determinism, gained ascendancy in the first half of the twentieth century, although it has since declined. Ivan Pavlov (d. 1936), Edward Thorndike (d. 1949), John Watson (d. 1958), and later the prolific Burrhus "Fred" Skinner (d. 1990) all based their work on controlled studies of animal behavior. For them, human freedom was illusory. Humans were basically conditioned beings, radically determined; if the patterns and details of their behavior, both individually and communally, could be minutely observed and tabulated, they would be shown to be fundamentally predictable.

Perhaps the best-known critic of Freud was the Swiss psychoanalyst Carl Jung (d. 1961), the founder of analytical psychology, for whom the key drive within humans was the need to establish individual identity. Like Freud, Jung focused on a patient's dreams, but he also considered them in relation to myths, art, spirituality, and beliefs. His most notable contribution was the concept of the psychological archetype and the collective unconscious. Jung emphasized the importance of balance and harmony, warning that people today rely too much on scientific and logical reasoning; they would benefit enormously from integrating spirituality and an appreciation of the unconscious. Jung's ideas found an echo in the remarkable Viktor Frankl (d. 1997), whose experiences in a Nazi concentration camp were determinative. A Viennese psychiatrist, Frankl pioneered "logotherapy," in which the spiritual drive and the human need for meaning and love are central to well-being. In his *The Doctor and the Soul* (1948) he asserted that "the salvation of man is through love and in love."

In the 1950s a complementary, more humanistic type of psychology began to emerge that explored human development, in part influenced by the then-current philosophies of personalism, phenomenology, and existentialism. By using phenomenology and first-person categories, the humanistic approach sought to treat patients holistically while focusing on such fundamental issues as self-identity, death, aloneness, freedom, and meaning. Thus Abraham Maslow (d. 1970) outlined the hierarchy of human needs, and Carl Rogers (d. 1987) developed "client-centered therapy," which used such techniques as nondirective counseling. One of the most notable developmental psychologists was Jean Piaget (d. 1980), who studied children and their cognitive development. Associated with him was Lawrence Kohlberg (d. 1987), who extended Piaget's work to moral development and outlined the structure and stages through which a person's moral development takes place; James Fowler, who, in his *Stages of Faith* (1981), applied all of this to a person's religious development; and Erik Erikson (d. 1994), who charted the stages of social development and is said to have coined the phrase "identity crisis."

Initially the church's magisterium was very cautious toward psychology. In the neoscholastic framework psychology was considered a branch of philosophy, and reconciling the new experimental psychology with the classical philosophical tradition presented serious intellectual challenges. Moreover, the new psychology seemed to be antireligious and based on materialist assumptions, while many psychologists believed psychology to be incompatible with Catholicism. Freud appeared to defy many traditional Catholic understandings of the human person: sin and guilt, moral freedom and responsibility, sexual morality. However, in the 1920s Cardinal Mercier, in the spirit of Leo XIII's *Aeterni Patris*, championed the new experimental psychology at KUL, seeking both to integrate its findings within a Thomistic framework and also to bring the insights of the Catholic and classical tradition to bear on psychology. Then, gradually, as psychology established itself and with the emergence of alternative schools of psychology and psychiatry, the initial caution began to yield. In 1948 the American Catholic Psychological Association was founded to represent Catholics working in psychology, to promote psychology in higher education, and to relate church teaching to psychology. While initially there were few Catholic psychologists in existence, by the 1960s the ACPA had over thirty thousand members. In the 1950s Pope Pius XII delivered three addresses on the moral aspects of psychological practice, which urged caution while giving an endorsement. Moreover, as Henryk Misiak and Virginia Staudt argued in their *Catholics in Psychology: A Historical Survey* (1954), the conviction was growing that experimental psychology, although it had developed from philosophy and therefore stood in some sort of relation to the classical tradition, should in fact be treated on its own terms as an autonomous human science. This position, which gained the ascendancy, effectively freed Catholic psychologists theoretically and practically from theology and philosophy departments. By the time of the Second Vatican Council, after decades of attempts to integrate psychology with Catholic thought, the goal seemed elusive at the very moment when psychology and psychoanalysis began to have a wider impact than ever upon society and within the church.

The influence of psychology today is felt especially within seminaries and houses of religious formation, particularly after John Paul II's Apostolic Exhortation on the Formation of Priests, *Pastores Dabo Vobis* (1992), which viewed human formation as "the basis of all priestly formation" (43). This document has radically transformed the nature, scope, and content of seminary formation and integrated the work of psychologists and counselors, men and women, into the formation of candidates. Psychologists and counselors now frequently assist on interview panels and assessment boards and are used at other times during seminary training. In the light of the clergy sexual-abuse crisis, as well as Vatican directives such as the Congregation for Catholic Education's *Instruction Concerning the Criteria for Discernment of Vocations with Regard to Persons with Homosexual Tendencies in View of Their Admission to the Seminary and Holy Orders* (2005), more specialized help is often offered to candidates as they prepare to make a lifelong commitment to chastity and celibacy. Indeed, human development in general has become a broad area of research within the church and can be seen operative, for instance, in the various North American *Institutes for the Study of Human Sexuality*.

The study of psychology is frequently of interest to pastors and religious. Many opt for in-service training courses on counseling or for further studies in psychology. Psychology has also influenced a number of recent Catholic spiritual writers. Thus the Franciscan Friar of Renewal and broadcaster Benedict Groeschel (b. 1933) brings together the insights of spirituality and psychology, as seen for instance in his *Spiritual Passages: The Psychology of Spiritual Development* (1983), which stresses the pivotal role of prayer and grace. The prolific Adrian van Kaam, CSSp, has developed his project of formative spirituality, which identifies the often implicit philosophical assumptions embedded in various psychological approaches and techniques, demonstrating how they affect theory and practice. Another popular spiritual writer, priest, and psychologist is John Powell, SJ, author of numerous books such as *Why Am I Afraid to Tell You Who I Am?* (1990). In this context mention might also be made of Jean Vanier (b. 1928), the founder of L'Arche, an international organization established on a combination of Christian principles and psychology that creates communities in which people with developmental difficulties and those who assist them can share life together. Finally, of a more strictly philosophical nature is the work of Robert Doran. Doran, heavily influenced by the philosophy of Lonergan, has focused on the relationship between psychology and philosophy. In his *Theology and the Dialectics of History* (1990) Doran could be said to have paved the way for the reunion of experimental psychology with the classical philosophical tradition, the point of convergence lying in what he terms "psychic conversion," an affective or symbolic shift that Lonergan himself confirmed was implicit in and consistent with his own thought.

However, even if Doran is correct in proposing the convergence of experimental psychology with Catholic thought within a richer and fuller anthropology, the general tension or dialectic between theology and psychology remains. Theology and psychology view the same human person, but in practice they do so from different starting points and with differing apparatus. They cannot be conflated. Holiness and wholeness are not the same thing, nor can it be presumed that what is spoken of in one is identical with something in the other, albeit with a different name. For instance, self-transcendence is not the same as self-realization, but actually the opposite. Again, to speak of what St. John of the Cross calls the "dark night of the soul" might in some manner be related to but cannot be treated as identical with the psychological states associated with clinical depression. In practice, psychology often supplants religion or smuggles into its procedures and therapies ethical stances and philosophical commitments at variance with theology. On the other hand, psychology is not itself a homogeneous whole but a disparate collection of studies. This is why the very project of integrating psychology with theology is elusive. Such a project would presume that psychology has a unity based on clearly developed presuppositions, which it evidently does not have. Consequently, from the perspective of Catholic theology the best to be hoped for from the psychologist is that the therapy fully respects sound anthropological, moral, and theological principles, while leaving the task of helping the patient to reach an integral theological view of what he or she has been undergoing to the spiritual director.

Analytical Philosophies

Analytical philosophy in its various forms is the family of philosophies now dominant in Anglo-American circles, and increasingly in continental Europe as well. Analytical approaches generally employ modern formal logic, which originated with Gottlob Frege (d. 1925) and which seeks to analyze the logical form of propositions. Its central concern is with clarity in the use of language, concepts, and argumentation, and it often goes with a positivism linked to the natural sciences. Analytical approaches concentrate on detail, usually eschewing any foundationalism that aspires to metaphysics or to a knowledge of the fundamental reasons and principles of things as a whole. Indeed, some analytical philosophers actively claim to defend common sense and ordinary language from the pretensions of metaphysics.

In this section our considerations will be limited to logical positivism and structuralism. Deconstructionalist thought will be postponed until later.

Linguistic analysis and logical positivism originated in the Vienna Circle of the 1920s. This was a group of philosophers who met regularly, often to discuss Ludwig Wittgenstein's *Tractatus*. They adopted the position that experience was the only source of knowledge and that logical analysis using symbolic logic was the chief method for resolving philosophical problems. The movement espoused verificationism: that is, the belief that the only meaningful propositions are those that are empirically demonstrable. Therefore they rejected metaphysics, religion, and aesthetics. The aim was to establish rigorous discourse, the strict analysis of terms, accuracy, and the isolation of anything that was absurd or redundant, thereby giving a secure scientific basis for statements.

Such concerns have also been highly in evidence in the philosophy departments of American universities in, for instance, the work of Willard Van Quine (d. 2000), the logician from Harvard, and also in Britain, where practitioners have reforged a link with the British Empiricist tradition. Thus at Cambridge, G. E. Moore (d. 1958), whose analysis predated the Vienna Circle, adopted a clear and methodical style while scrutinizing ethical reasoning and the use of common sense, and Bertrand Russell (d. 1970), mathematician, social reformer, and an implacable opponent of religion, wrote about the philosophy of science. At Oxford, Sir A. J. ("Freddie") Ayer (d. 1989) became associated with the promotion of the Verification Principle, although he later modified his rigorist position, and at the London School of Economics the Austrian-born Karl Popper (d. 1994), one of the most distinguished philosophers of science of the twentieth century, proposed the theory of falsification: that nothing not logically demonstrable is rationally coherent. Mention should also be made here—although he is in a class of his own—of the enigmatic Austrian-born Ludwig Wittgenstein (d. 1951), who spent much of his life in Manchester and Cambridge. As a youth in the Austrian army he underwent mystical experiences, thoughts from which he wrote up in his *Tractatus Logico-Philosophicus* (1921). This latter famously treats of the limits of language: "whereof we cannot speak, thereon we must remain silent." His later work, the *Philosophical Investigations*, completed in Cambridge but translated and published posthumously by Elizabeth Anscombe in 1953, revealed subtle changes in his thought. It explored semantics, logic, the philosophy of mathematics, and the philosophy of mind, and identified the various language games operative in human discourse, diagnosing the root cause of many philosophical problems as conceptual confusions caused by language. Wittgenstein influenced a number of subsequent thinkers such as Peter Winch (d. 1997), who applied his thought to the social sciences, ethics, and religion.

Recently some analytical philosophers have "rediscovered" metaphysics. Thus Peter Strawson (d. 2006), a critic of Bertrand Russell, piloted the project of "descriptive metaphysics" and developed the notion of shared concepts operative in everyday life. Another, Richard Rorty (d. 2007), who had a comprehensive understanding of the analytical tradition, famously rejected that tradition out of frustration with its apparent narrowness. "Converting" to continental philosophy, he studied the work of Martin Heidegger, Michel Foucault, and Jacques Derrida, through whom he tried to bridge the gap between the analytical and continental traditions and to demonstrate their complementarity.

One of the numerous and disparate strands of analytical philosophy is structuralism, which seeks to explore how the structural relationships between concepts and principles in language and literature vary between different mental, linguistic, and cultural structures, with the belief that these relationships can be usefully exposed and explored. Ferdinand de Saussure (d. 1913), the Swiss linguist who laid the foundation for many of the most significant developments in linguistic analysis in the twentieth century, saw language as basically a culturally conditioned sign system signifying meaning. For him, reality was unknowable and undifferentiated: everything depended on perspective, or more specifically, the perspective of the culture and language group to which the viewer belongs, and so different language groups relate to different realities.

Other thinkers included the American scholar Charles Sanders Peirce (d. 1914), whose thought on logic and semiotics became influential in the mid-twentieth century; Noam Chomsky (b. 1928), the American psychologist mentioned above who has worked on "generative linguistics"; and Claude Lévi-Strauss (b. 1908), a follower of Émile Durkheim (d. 1917), the father of sociology and anthropology, and who in turn influenced a number of subsequent thinkers, some of whom appear below in the section on late modernism. Lévi-Strauss's studies of myth and its structures demonstrated the remarkable similarity between the various myths of very differing cultures. However, in the 1980s, with the emergence of deconstructionalism, some of Lévi-Strauss's protégés went on to become "post-structuralists" who rejected some of structuralism's key tenets. These included Roland Barthes (d. 1980), who worked on semiotics and the structures of literary criticism; Jacques Lacan (d. 1981), the Freudian psychologist already mentioned who saw language as central to psychology but who rejected the structuralist claim that meaning is independent of culture; and Michel Foucault (d. 1984), who claimed to have exposed the structural connection between knowledge and power, arguing for dissolution.

Structuralism has had a general and pervasive impact on many areas of biblical exegesis. It has served more as a mind-set for exegetes than an explicit philosophical partner as they have striven to identify links with common ancient Near Eastern myths and with Jewish traditions.

Bengt Holmberg (b. 1942), in his *Paul and Power* (1980), exposes some of the power struggles that allegedly took place within the early Christian communities, while Xavier Léon-Dufour, one of the foremost French New Testament scholars (cf. his 1987 *Sharing the Eucharistic Bread*), has identified links between the early church and its Jewish matrix. Structuralist concerns and the notion of symbolic language are important also in Pierre Grelot's *The Language of Symbolism: Biblical Theology, Semantics, and Exegesis* (2006). Moreover, as a conscious or unconscious mind-set structuralism has also pervaded the study of church history. If, as structuralism suggests, all truth is created by the group that utters it, the statements of church councils are the result less of the common pursuit of truth through debate than of the greater power of the party or faction that ultimately prevailed. On this premise scholars and historians such as Norman Tanner, Richard Costigan, and Paul Christophe have explored afresh the events of church history and the manner in which the various factions, tensions, debates, and outcomes of councils and papal statements occurred.

Linguistic analysis and logical positivism are often related to empiricism, the claim that the only sure knowledge is what can be empirically verified. Positivism purports to deny those things that cannot be known through the senses. While these may not seem to be promising dialogue partners for Catholic theology, recent theology has nonetheless begun to take analytical concerns seriously.

The issue for theology is the need to espouse high standards of discourse that eschew the nonrational. There are now a number of "analytical Thomists," that is, thinkers who have originated from, or rediscovered elements of, the Thomist and scholastic tradition and who draw on classical philosophy's emphasis on clarity in order to deal not so much with systematic theology as with the philosophy of religion. Mention should be made here of such Polish logicians of the lvov-Warsaw school as Stanisław Jaśkowski (d. 1965), Tadeusz Czeżowski (d. 1981), and Joseph Bochenski (d. 1995); and also in Britain of Anthony Kenny (b. 1931), who has written about the philosophy of mind, philosophy of religion, and Wittgenstein; and Peter Geach (b. 1916), who has presented aspects of the thought of Aquinas in the style of modern philosophy.

Other scholars include Peter Geach's wife Elizabeth Anscombe (d. 2001), the Wittgensteinian philosopher, and the Dominican scholars Fergus Kerr, author of *Theology after Wittgenstein* (1986) and *After Aquinas* (2002), and Thomist specialist Brian Davies (b. 1951). Mention should also be made of the prominent legal philosopher John Finnis (b. 1940), whose

Natural Law and Natural Rights (1979) is regarded as one of the definitive modern works on natural law philosophy. In it Finnis brings together both Oxford and Thomistic traditions in order to challenge Anglo-American positivism. All of these thinkers, predominantly philosophers who draw on analytical approaches and who espouse clear discourse, have in the course of their work made contributions to theology. This is the context in which British Catholic theologians such as Nicholas Lash (b. 1934), John Haldane (b. 1954), and Margaret Atkins (b. 1969) write.

Philosophies of History, Social Change, and Hermeneutics

Under this catchall umbrella of philosophies of history, social change, and hermeneutics are grouped a number of philosophical movements that came to the fore in the mid-twentieth century, all related to history, society, development, and hermeneutics. These include process philosophy, philosophies of history, and theories of interpretation.

Process Philosophy

Not all contemporary philosophers have come to a negative appraisal of metaphysics. Some have sought to relate metaphysics to contemporary concerns, making change and evolution central, and reenvisaging Being in more dynamic categories. In the classical tradition metaphysics was generally understood to be timeless, concerned with substance, objects, and things, while downplaying or subordinating processes. However, process philosophy intentionally reverses this priority. It purports to have transcended the static character of the Aristotelian-Thomist tradition and made becoming and change the cornerstone of ontology.

The notion of change at the heart of reality goes back to Heraclitus and early Hellenistic thought, but process thought was given impetus as the basis for a new metaphysics by Henri Bergson (d. 1941). In his *Creative Evolution* (1907) Bergson spoke of an *élan vitale*, a vital force, pulsing through matter and also through humans as a source of creativity, as the explanation of evolution and the development of organisms. Another type of process can be discerned in the writings of Pierre Teilhard de Chardin (d. 1955), theologian and palaeontologist. His posthumously published *The Phenomenon of Man* (1958) proposed orthogenesis, the teleological view that evolution occurs in a directional, goal-driven manner, unfolding from matter to cell to organism and then to the emergence of the noosphere or consciousness. In humanity evolution has now taken a spiritual form, shown in the incarnation of Christ, and is progressing toward the Omega Point (or moment of "Christogenesis") in the future. But it is probably the British-born philosopher and mathematician Alfred North Whitehead (d. 1947) who is most associated with process thinking. In his *Process and Reality* (1929) Whitehead attempted to synthesize religion and science, proposing a dynamic metaphysics in which everything is in the process of becoming, including God. What goes on in the world also really and truly affects God, and vice versa. Whitehead had studied Bergson but was particularly struck by the collapse of Newtonian physics in the early twentieth century. In his later *The Adventures of Ideas* (1933) he went on to provide new process definitions of beauty, truth, art, adventure, and peace, while his ideas found subsequent resonances in a number of scientific realms, including cosmological theories about the Big Bang: that the universe began at a particular point in time in a simple state and has subsequently grown ever more complex.

These diverse forms of process philosophy have inspired process theologies or theologies in some way associated with progress. Thus Teilhard de Chardin, although officially disfavored by Rome for allegedly undermining the doctrine of original sin, nevertheless captured the *Zeitgeist* of Catholic theology in the 1950s and 1960s, his thought becoming entwined with the progressivist currents at Vatican II. His ideas have inspired a new concern with cosmology and a renewed theological response to evolutionary theories. Teilhard's thought has been discussed and challenged by a wide range of subsequent theologians, and notably by Walter Ong, SJ (d. 2003). Moreover, he has also inspired countless artists and litterateurs working in a wide range of media, such as the Catholic authors and novelists Flannery O'Connor (d. 1964) and Maurice West (d. 1999); the science-fiction writer Julian May (b. 1931); the convert British musician and composer Edmund Rubbra (d. 1986), whose *Symphony No. 8* (1968) was titled *Hommage a Teilhard de Chardin*; and the Catholic sculptor Frederick Hart (d. 1999), creator of the acrylic *Divine Milieu: Homage to Teilhard de Chardin* (2001).

Process metaphysics, moreover, has sired "process theology." These new theologies of God articulate a new understanding of his presence and activity in the world. They have begun to appear in Catholic theology, as in *Evolutionary Faith* (2002), *Quantum Theology* (2004), and the other writings of the Sacred Heart missionary Diarmuid O'Murchu (b. 1952), and also in the works of the liberation theologian Jon Sobrino. The latter's *Christology at the Crossroads* (1978) depicted a God truly united with the sufferings of the poor, even arguably to the extent of "patripassionism"

(God the Father suffering on the cross). But the influence of process thought has been more evident in Protestant and Reformed theology. A notable exponent was Charles Hartshorne (d. 2000), whose *A Natural Theology for Our Time* (1967) proposed panentheism (all is in God). In Hartshorne's theology God is neither identical with the world nor completely independent from it. God can change because God and the world exist in a dynamic, changing relationship. God has a self-identity that transcends the world, but like a fetus within its mother, the world, which has a kind of "dependent independency," is also contained within God. Hartshorne finds proof for his assertions about the mutability of God in the Bible, where at times God seems to become angry, change his mind, or react to events.

Some process theologians discuss God's omnipotence, its extent, and its limits—whether, for instance, God is not omnipotent in the sense of being coercive but rather has the divine power of persuasion. Others stress the role of agents of free will in determining the universe, and this extends to God. God has a will in everything, but not everything that occurs is God's will. The American Methodist theologian John Cobb in his *For the Common Good: Redirecting the Economy toward Community, the Environment, and a Sustainable Future* (1989) applies Whiteheadian metaphysics to social justice and economic issues. Another practitioner is the feminist theologian Sallie McFague (b. 1937), who in her *Models of God: Theology for an Ecological, Nuclear Age* (1987) and *The Body of God: An Ecological Theology* (1993) analyzed contemporary models for God, opting for the ecological model of the world as the body of God. Still others, such as David Ray Griffin (b. 1939) and Philip Clayton (b. 1957), deal with key aspects of process theology such as the interconnected nature of reality, the subjectivity of science, the immanence and transcendence of God, the synthesis of science and religion, and how God responds to creation with creativity.

Philosophies of History

Now we consider the influence on theology of another type of change, namely, historical change or, in more general terms, the impact on theology of modern historiography and historical scholarship. Akin to the endeavor to see metaphysics in more dynamic categories has been the attempt to view epistemology in more dynamic categories, and in particular for theology to take seriously the modern sense of historical awareness.

We have already discussed the historical differentiation within theology and, particularly with the eclipse of neoscholasticism after Vatican II, the impact on Catholic theology of historical consciousness, the sense of history that came to the fore with the Enlightenment and pervades modernity. One thinker who developed a profound philosophical reflection on this was Bernard Lonergan. Lonergan's thought on history was influenced by the English historian Christopher Dawson (d. 1970) and his *The Age of the Gods* (1928) on cultural history and Christendom, and Paul Hazard (d. 1944), who in his *The European Mind* (1952) studied the major developments that occurred with the French revolution. Lonergan, painting with broad brushstrokes, argued that Western culture had undergone in recent times a profound cultural shift from classical to modern—and to postmodern, some would now add—controls of meaning, and this overlaying of the old with the new is visible in every area of human endeavor from music, art, and literature to poetry, philosophy, and theology. Modernity, unlike the classical, does not see itself as normative and fixed, but as plastic, relative, and developing. Where the classical was a fusion of Greek philosophy and Roman juridical, military, and practical organization, with the Judeo-Christian religion reaching its zenith in the Gothic of the High Middle Ages, the modern is based on the new anthropocentric and rationalistic philosophies of the Enlightenment, empirical science, and secularism. The rise of modern science has now been accompanied also by the rise of modern critical scholarship.

This cultural shift, according to Lonergan, has presented an enormous challenge. Catholicism was so successfully and deeply wedded to the classical culture that it baptized it, and Christianity deeply imbibed the thought forms and expressions of classicism in its liturgy, organization, and thought. From the nineteenth century onward, however, new and far-reaching questions were being put to the tradition (e.g., the new historical-critical methods of interpreting the Scriptures), which the church resisted until the mid-twentieth century, with waning success. Consequently, in Lonergan's view, when Vatican II used the key word *aggiornamento* it was calling for a gradual, careful, yet thorough disengagement from classicism and the transposition of doctrine, life, and worship into the categories of modernity:

> Classical culture cannot be jettisoned without being replaced; and what replaces it cannot but run counter to classical expectation. There is bound to be formed a solid right that is determined to live in a world that no longer exists. There is bound to be formed a scattered

> left, captivated now by this now by that new development, exploring now this and now that new possibility. But what will count is a perhaps not numerous centre, big enough to be at home in both the old and the new, painstaking enough to work out one by one the transitions to be made, strong enough to refuse half measures and insist on complete solutions even though it has to wait. (Bernard Lonergan, "Dimensions of Meaning," in *Collection*, 245)

It is this activity of disengagement, Lonergan averred, that more than anything has created a sense of crisis within the church, a crisis not of faith but of culture.

Lonergan's account of cultural shift was taken up widely in postconciliar theology, notably by David Tracy (b. 1939). Leslie Dewart, in his *The Future of Belief* (1966), argued that theologians now needed to "de-Hellenize" the church's thinking by abandoning concepts of God derived from Greek and medieval philosophy that are out of accord with contemporary human experience. Peter Chirico, notably in his *Infallibility: The Crossroads of Doctrine* (1977); Thomas Rausch (b. 1942) in his *Towards a Truly Catholic Church: An Ecclesiology for the Third Millennium* (2005); and Richard McBrien (b. 1936), author of *Catholicism* (1994), a popular college-level introduction to Catholic Christianity, have all made Lonergan's account of cultural shift central to a renewed understanding of ecclesiology. Ladislas Örsy (b. 1921) has applied it creatively to canon law. Richard Gula (b. 1953), author of *Reason Informed by Faith: Foundations of Catholic Morality* (1989), Charles Curran, and others have grounded new directions in moral theology on the notion of cultural shift.

Lonergan's account was subtle, yet open textured. Not surprisingly, it was contested and/or misunderstood. Charles Davis (d. 1999), the British theologian and author of *A Question of Conscience* (1967), seeing in Lonergan a warrant to reject what he believed to be outmoded traditions, said, "I would never have been able to leave the Roman Catholic Church but for my reading of Lonergan." Others, such as Tracey Rowland (b. 1963) in her *Culture and the Thomist Tradition: After Vatican II* (2003) have interpreted Lonergan to mean that "what the church gained from her inculturation in the world of Greco-Latin thought and culture" must now be abandoned (45). Because it historically lacked a theological critique of culture, Catholicism, according to Rowland, has taken on the new forms of modernity, particularly in the liturgy, in an uncritical manner, while the classical forms—the Catholic traditions of music, art, liturgical development, prayer, and devotion—were emptied out and discarded without proper attention to their abiding meaning and value. She blames Lonergan, among others, for theologically legitimating this. However, it could also be argued that Lonergan stressed the need for a "critical" transposition since he saw the normativity of classical culture as deriving from its Christian "baptism." Moreover, John Paul II spoke of the permanent achievements of the classical inheritance that presumably need not be transposed but rediscovered (*Fides et Ratio* 72) and Benedict XVI, while recognizing that the church itself is a cultural subject, has pointed out that the encounter between the biblical message and Greek philosophy was not an accident but divinely willed (*Address at Regensburg University*, 2006).

THEORIES OF INTERPRETATION AND SOCIAL THEORY

Another issue here among the philosophies of change is that of critical theory, theories of interpretation, the correct method of hermeneutics, and the use of historical methods. Obviously this is important in investigating the reliability and meaning of ancient texts (higher and lower criticism, internal evidences, etc.), but issues of interpretation arise across the board in historical studies. Wilhelm Dilthey (d. 1911), who drew on Hegel, was one of the first to explore this. His initial aim was to find the philosophical foundations for historical studies and for what he called the "sciences of man, of society, and of the state," the *Geisteswissenschaften* or human sciences of history, philosophy, religion, psychology, art, literature, law, politics, and economics. Other key figures included the neo-Kantian philosophers of religion and culture, Ernst Troeltsch (d. 1923), who claimed that all religious truth claims were subject to historical contingencies—hence the complaint sometimes heard of "Troeltschean relativism"—and Georg Simmel (d. 1918), one of the founders of sociology. Karl Mannheim (d. 1947) developed a comprehensive sociological analysis of the structures of knowledge, and Thomas Kuhn (d. 1996), the historian and philosopher of science, in his influential *The Structure of Scientific Revolutions* (1962) popularized the idea of "paradigm shifts" in knowledge and the use of "models."

Mention should also be made here of the giant figure of Hans-Georg Gadamer (d. 2002), best known for his *Truth and Method* (1960), in which he proposed the use of the "hermeneutic circle" as the necessary key to correct interpretation, leading to a "fusing of horizons" (a *Horizonsgeschmeltzung*). Gadamer was in part influenced by the thought of Karl Jaspers (d. 1969), who, like Heidegger, explored human being (*Sein*) and existence (*Dasein*), and who sought to reconstruct a common horizon between science, religion, and common sense. His intention was to secure a transcendent basis from which to construct a social and political critique. Gadamer had a great influence both on his contemporaries and on subsequent philosophers, notably Paul Ricoeur (d. 2005), who combined phenomenological description with hermeneutical interpretation.

Mention has already been made of Marxism and other critical social research and theories. Here we might note the Frankfurt School, founded in 1929, which originally comprised philosophers such as Max Horkheimer (d. 1973), who set the agenda by analyzing democratic institutions, politics, the family, and modern culture; Theodor Adorno (d. 1969), author of the pessimistic *The Dialectic of Enlightenment* (1941) on modern reason and freedom; the psychoanalyst Eric Fromm (d. 1980); later the great Jürgen Habermas (b. 1929), best known for his work on social theory and the concept of the public sphere; and Hannah Arendt (d. 1975), the political theorist who discussed the nature of power and authority. In 2004 Habermas famously engaged in a public debate with the then-Cardinal Ratzinger in which the two of them reached a remarkable consensus on the roles of reason and faith within a free and secular society.

All of these diverse and loosely historicist schools of philosophy concerned with the social theory and the nature of knowledge, with hermeneutics and theories of interpretation, have had a pervasive impact on recent theology, particularly on the liberal strands of Protestant theology but also on postconciliar Catholic theology. Already in the nineteenth century the Tübingen School, typified by the ecclesiologist Johann Adam Möhler (d. 1838) and, in England, John Henry Newman (d. 1890), were keenly aware of the historicity of knowledge in general and theological knowledge in particular. With Newman and his 1845 *Essay on the Development of Christian Doctrine*, Catholic theology began the momentous process of coming to terms with history, permanence, and change, especially with regard to doctrine. These nineteenth-century concerns re-emerged as an explosive problematic in the post–*Humanae Vitae* period. This can be seen in the number of works published in the 1970s relating to doctrinal development, such as *Unfolding Revelation: The Nature of Doctrinal Development* (1972) by Jan Walgrave (b. 1911), *Dogma: The Church, Its Origin and Structure* (1972) by Michael Schmaus, *Change in Focus: A Study of Doctrinal Change and Continuity* (1973) by Nicholas Lash, *Has Dogma a Future?* (1975) by Gerald O'Collins, *Models of the Church* by Avery Dulles (d. 2008), and *Blessed Rage for Order* (1975) by David Tracy.

Again, the impact of modern historical-critical methods on Catholic biblical exegesis, postponed for almost two centuries, was encouraged by the 1943 encyclical of Pius XII, *Divino Afflante Spiritu*, promoting biblical studies. The use of these methods has raised questions among biblical scholars about theories of interpretation and what would constitute an authentic hermeneutical method. The 1993 PBC document *The Interpretation of the Bible in the Church* attempted to suggest parameters and guidelines. Interestingly, it began with a critical survey of all the chief methods of exegesis and hermeneutics currently in use—the historical-critical, the new methods of literary analysis, tradition-based approaches, the use of the human sciences (sociology, cultural anthropology, psychology, and psychoanalysis), contextual approaches (liberationist and feminist), and fundamentalism—before going on to discuss hermeneutical issues and the characteristics of what it saw as authentic interpretation. Hermeneutical issues have been extensively discussed by feminist theologians but also by other scholars such as William Kurz (b. 1939), author of *Reading Luke-Acts: The Dynamics of Biblical Narrative* (1993); Ben Meyer (d. 1995), who wrote *Critical Realism and the New Testament* (1989) and *Reality and Illusion in New Testament Scholarship* (1994); and Sean McEvenue, who has published a number of books and articles on interpretation, not least *Interpretation and Bible: Essays on Truth in Literature* (1994).

The specialization of church history has undergone a renaissance in recent times with the publication of various revisionist treatments of the English Reformation, notably Eamon Duffy's *The Stripping of the Altars* (1992) and *The Voices of Morebath: Reformation and Rebellion in an English Village* (2001). There has also been a resurgence of interest in the nineteenth century, typified by a number of new biographies of the important ecclesiastics of the time, including *William Bernard Ullathorne: A Different Kind of Monk* (2006) by Judith Champ (b. 1953). Much of this interest has centered on a rediscovery of the biography, writings, and theology of John Henry Newman, not least because so many of his foundational ideas came to the fore during the Second Vatican Council and its aftermath. As the English Benedictine theologian Bishop Christopher Butler (d. 1986) once put it: "Newman's spirit brooded over the council." In recent years there has been a veritable explosion of Newman scholarship, including the magisterial *John Henry Newman: A Biography* (1990) by Ian Ker (b. 1945); the study of his philosophy, *Newman's Approach to Knowledge* (2004) by Laurence Richardson; and studies of his theology such as *Clear Heads and Holy Hearts: The Religious and Theological Ideal of John Henry*

Newman (1991) by Terrence Merrigan, and *John Henry Newman* (2002) by Avery Dulles.

In fact, to speak in the most general terms, a strong sense of historical perspective now pervades every domain of Catholic theology. This is in marked contrast to the thesis theology and theological tracts dominant during the neoscholastic period.

Late-modernism/Postmodernism

Are we now at the end or at a beginning? In other words, is postmodernity the logical conclusion of the Enlightenment and the trajectory of thought it initiated? Or is postmodern thought the beginning of a new way of looking at things that over time will itself flourish and diversify?

Postmodern movements run in opposite directions. "Deconstructionism" and "anti-foundationalism" are probably the best known, representing the inevitable conclusion of the critique Kant initiated, namely, that all knowledge is subjective, fallible, and fragmented. Metaphysics, foundations, and "grand narratives" are impossible. This *fin de siècle* mood pervading media, entertainment, architecture, music, and the arts has been explored philosophically by such thinkers as Jacques Derrida (d. 2004), who coined the term "deconstruction" in the 1960s, and Jean Francois Lyotard (d. 1998), the literary theorist, who in his *The Postmodern Condition: A Report on Knowledge* (1979) first articulated the spirit of postmodernism and its impact on the human condition. Lyotard, who was implacably opposed to universals, metanarratives, generality, and critical of many of the universalist claims of the Enlightenment, modified Wittgenstein's account of language games and argued instead for difference, diversity, and the micronarrative. Others in this group included Derrida's one-time student Jean-Luc Marion (b. 1946), who in *God Without Being* analyzed idolatry, love, and gift while proclaiming the end of metaphysics, and Michel Foucault (d. 1984), who disclosed the social power play behind universals. In all these respects deconstructionism marks the end of the road from the Enlightenment.

Other seams of postmodern philosophy, however, involve a postliberal reaction against modernity and the culture that emerged with the Enlightenment. Precritical approaches attempt in some manner to return to the pre-Enlightenment era, and these are often in vogue in fundamentalist and neoconservative movements. Thus the British philosopher Alasdair MacIntyre (b. 1929), now a Catholic and a Thomist, in his *After Virtue* (1981) and *Whose Justice? Which Rationality?* (1988) portrayed modern society as a collection of individuals washed up on a desert island, needing to recover the common language of a tradition in order to survive. A critic of modernity, MacIntyre has become central to current interest in virtue ethics, that is, the development of the moral life through habits and virtues. The ethicist Stanley Hauerwas has adopted a similar intellectual *iter*, seeking to "drive behind" modernity in order to reconnect with and recover for today the perennial truths of classical wisdom. Others adopt postcritical approaches that take account of the insights of modernity while seeking to move beyond it. Thus Jürgen Habermas rejected the pessimism of postmodernist thought, arguing that the Enlightenment project should be corrected, not discarded, if a more humane, just, and egalitarian society based on reason is to be established, and Paul Ricoeur, while accepting the modern critical need for a hermeneutics of suspicion undergirding all investigation, also argued for a complementary hermeneutics of recovery.

Postmodern philosophies have influenced Catholic theology in a number of ways. While Catholic theologians generally eschew the disregard for universals shown in the deconstructionist and anti-foundationalist strands of postmodernism—it could be argued that John Paul II in *Fides et Ratio* sought precisely to bolster philosophical confidence in the ability of human reason to make such metaphysical assertions—many have become sensitive in their writings to the metanarrative and foundationalist claims that Catholic theology wishes to make. This is evident, for instance, in the later writings of Heinrich Fries, notably in his *Fundamental Theology* (1996). Moreover, current research as seen in journals seems to favor particularity and analysis over generalization and global perspectives; this contrasts with previous theology, particularly scholastic and patristic theology, which always had an "architectonic" sense to it, as if the immediate issue was being treated against a universal perspective, the entire Christian mystery being present in the midst of the detail. On the other hand, there has also been a move in favor of narrative and artistic approaches to theology, ostensibly based on the manner in which Christ used parables and stories in the Scriptures. The Jesuit spiritual writer John Navone (b. 1930), author of the classic *Towards a Theology of Story* (1977), in particular has developed this. Mention should also be made of narrative theology, sometimes called post-liberal theology, associated with the Yale school of Hans Frei (d. 1988), Stanley Hauerwas, and George Lindbeck (b. 1923). Lindbeck, in his *The Nature of Doctrine: Religion and Theology in a Postliberal Age* (1984), proposed a cultural-linguistic approach in which doctrines were to be seen not as truth claims but as authoritative rules of discourse, attitude, and action in and for the Christian community.

Perennial Philosophy

For the sake of completeness, we return here to the impact on recent Catholic theology of the *philosophia perennis*, the broad classical tradition of philosophy comprising neo-Platonism, Augustinianism, and Thomism, plus "common sense" thought.

It is worth recalling here some of the reasons why Leo XII had found Thomism and the classical tradition useful: their tried and tested presentation of Catholicism, their realism that took into account the incarnation, their useful distinction between the natural and the supernatural—although this was much debated in the mid-twentieth century, notably between Karl Rahner and Henri de Lubac—and their account of the *praeambula fidei*, including natural theology and apologetical arguments for the existence of God. In all this, Thomism apparently met the requirements of *Dei Filius* regarding the relationship of faith and reason. However, as the twentieth century progressed it was perceived to be increasingly problematic. Thomism seemed out of step with the *Zeitgeist*, unresponsive to the events of the century, particularly the world wars and advances in science, medicine, and technology, and lacking an effective philosophy of history and culture. Its juridical imposition, blended with the anti-modernist suspicions of the era, resulted in growing complexity as theologians tried to demonstrate their Thomistic pedigree while reaching into other streams of thought. This led in turn to conflict between a number of the more progressive theologians of the time—such as Henri de Lubac, Marie-Dominique Chenu, Yves Congar, and Karl Rahner—with their superiors as well as with Rome. Further, the different schools or strands within Thomism became radicalized. Consequently, by the late 1950s, the biblical and patristic revival together with the engagement of more personalist, phenomenological, existentialist, and historical approaches began to outshine Thomism. This is still largely the case today.

Evidently, contemporary Catholic theology is a philosophical smorgasbord. Yet the classical tradition still remains the main, if somewhat "diluted," dialogue partner for Catholic theology. It still forms the broad tradition across most domains of theology, from catechetics and ecclesiology to morals and canon law, with the notable exception of biblical, patristic, and historical theology. Mention might be made of Christoph Schönborn (b. 1945), director of the project that led to the *Catechism of the Catholic Church* (1994) and author of the four-volume *Living the Cate-chism of the Catholic Church* (1995–2003), which reemphasizes doctrine and the realities of faith rather than personal experience and subjective meaning, and also the two moral theologians Servais Pinckaers and Jean Porter (b. 1955). The latter's *Nature as Reason: A Thomistic Theory of the Natural Law* (2005) develops a new theory of natural law relevant to current concerns yet based on elements of Aquinas. Moreover, there has been a recent revival of interest in Augustine. This is evident in the writings of Joseph Ratzinger, but also in the emergence of Radical Orthodoxy, a self-styled postmodern group of theologians, mainly Anglican, who have revived an Augustinian Thomism in order to recall theology to more orthodox lines, while strongly critiquing modernity and liberalism. The foundational work of this group was the collection of essays titled *Radical Orthodoxy: A New Theology* (1999) by John Milbank, Catherine Pickstock, and Graham Ward (b. 1955).

Chapter Four

Theological Method

Having established and explored the relationship of philosophy to theology (chapter 1), we surveyed recent Catholic theology (chapter 2) and the influence on it of contemporary philosophies (chapter 3). We now conclude with a brief study of the "philosophy of theology," that is, the structure and division of theology, its methods, some of its features, and its current styles.

1. The Structures of Theology

In general it is true to say that the structures and methods of theology were not systematically explored until the Middle Ages, while method itself has only become a problem in the modern era. However, in the early period councils and synods with their professions of faith or creeds played an important "normative" role within theology. In the medieval period theology became more systematic, thanks to the method of the *quaestio disputata*. The Reformation led to the emergence of the catechism. After the Enlightenment, thesis-theology reversed the approach of the *quaestio* in favor of dogmatic answers. Today the demise of neoscholasticism at Vatican II, together with the pluralism, creativity, and specialization of contemporary theology, has created something of a methodological crisis in theology.

Early Theological Methods: The Profession of Faith

In the first millennium theology straightforwardly took the form that seemed to be needed or that suggested itself. Thus in the New Testament era theology was, as noted above using the phrase of Terry Tekippe, a

123

"thematization of Christian experience," that is, a reflective account of the Christian's lived ecclesial experience of Jesus Christ and the Gospel. Writers recorded their experience of Christ and reflected on how his message might be lived within the Christian community. Paul sent letters and instructions to the churches he founded. The Acts of the Apostles recorded the spread of the early church. The gospels recounted the life of Christ, the Synoptics mediating the message to the Jewish world, John to the Hellenistic. In the subapostolic era Christians needed to demonstrate to the Jews that Christ was the fulfillment of Old Testament expectations and to defend their beliefs against some of the pagan philosophies of the Roman Empire. This led, respectively, to commentaries on Scripture and apologetical writings. In the fourth century, new theological forms emerged that included sermons, meditations on Scripture and the sayings of Jesus, autobiographies such as Augustine's *Confessions*, accounts of church history, and catechetical tracts.

However, what was significant from this time onward was the formal development within theology of doctrinal differentiation. This was the era of the great councils and synods. The need to distinguish the permanent truths of faith (i.e., doctrine) from error and to determine the extent and limits of ecclesial communion led to conciliar statements and decrees, pronouncements and canons, plus the baptismal and creedal statements. It could be argued that, after the Scriptures themselves, the single most important determinant of the theological methods of the first millennium was the development of creedal formularies: short, pithy formulas expressing the church's faith and authoritatively promulgated by church councils and synods. These creeds and the statements of the councils and synods that articulated them—the magisterium—would henceforth play a normative role within Western theology, guiding and directing its endeavors.

The origins of the creeds are complex (see figure 7). They go back in all probability to the "cross-fertilization" in the second and third centuries of two features from the New Testament era. One was the christological faith formula, a kerygmatic saying that summarized the Christian faith. In the Scriptures these took three forms: "Jesus is Lord" (e.g., 1 Cor 12:3), "Jesus is the Christ" (e.g., Acts 2:36), and "Jesus is the Son of God" (e.g., Acts 9:20). Over time these basic confessions became embellished with the events of Christ's death and resurrection and their significance. For instance, Paul says:

> I handed on to you as of first importance what I in turn had received:
> that Christ died for our sins in accordance with the Scriptures, and

that he was buried, and that he was raised on the third day in accordance with the Scriptures, and that he appeared to Cephas, then to the twelve. (1 Cor 15:3-5)

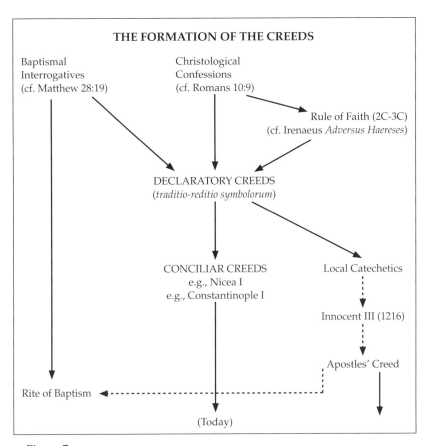

THE FORMATION OF THE CREEDS

Figure 7

The other feature from the early church at the origin of the creeds was the "baptismal interrogative" used in the rite of baptism, the formula of a Trinitarian question and answer. These were along the lines suggested in the Gospel of Matthew:

> Go therefore and make disciples of all nations, baptizing them in the name of the Father and of the Son and of the Holy Spirit, and teaching them to obey everything that I have commanded you. (Matt 28:19)

Early examples of such baptismal questions and answers can be found in Justin Martyr (*Apologia* I.61), in Tertullian, who speaks of a triple immersion in water after each interrogative (*De Corona Militis* 3), and in the *Apostolic Tradition* of Hippolytus:

> When each of them to be baptized has gone down into the water, the one baptizing shall lay hands on each of them, asking, "Do you believe in God the Father Almighty?" And the one being baptized shall answer, "I believe." He shall then baptize each of them once, laying his hand upon each of their heads. Then he shall ask, "Do you believe in Jesus Christ, the Son of God, who was born of the Holy Spirit and the Virgin Mary, who was crucified under Pontius Pilate, and died, and rose on the third day living from the dead, and ascended into heaven, and sat down at the right hand of the Father, the one coming to judge the living and the dead?" When each has answered, "I believe," he shall baptize a second time. Then he shall ask, "Do you believe in the Holy Spirit and the Holy Church and the resurrection of the flesh?" Then each being baptized shall answer, "I believe." And thus let him baptize the third time. (Hippolytus, *Apostolic Tradition* 21:12-18: cf. ND 2)

In the second and third centuries there seems to have been a cross-fertilization of the confession of faith with the baptismal interrogative. This can be seen in the theological principle of the *regula fidei*, the rule or canon of faith, a notional summary of Christian doctrine and the basic doctrinal tradition of the church, believed to be consonant with what had been handed down from the apostles. This rule of faith was not a written rule but rather something believed by Christians in the heart, although Irenaeus and other authors occasionally describe it (see *Adversus Haereses* III.4.1). Also in the third century, with new and more elaborate catechetical programs for baptism, there developed a practice of a *traditio et reditio symbolorum* (lit. the handing out and the return of symbols) in the last stages of the catechumenate, a feature restored in the modern *Rite of Christian Initiation of Adults*. A summary of faith was given to the catechumen to learn and study over a period of time, before he or she "handed it back" to the bishop in a personal and public profession of faith during the last weeks of Lent. A number of these declaratory creeds are extant from the third and fourth centuries. They are in essence positive versions of the baptismal interrogatory creeds and include the Old Roman Creed, which was known and used by Ambrose of Milan (d. 397), and the Apostles' Creed, a later reformulation of the Old Roman Creed that eventually settled into the twelve theological statements we have today. It is used on occasion in the Western eucharistic liturgy and in question and answer form in the Western rite of baptism.

The final stage in the historical evolution of the creeds came in the fourth century with the pressing need for the church to lay down orthodox doctrine clearly and to determine ecclesial communion. The immediate challenges came from the christological and trinitarian controversies of the time. The councils and synods called to deal with these challenges issued conciliar creeds and creedal statements based on the baptismal symbols, but written in a first person plural, declarative format: "We believe," not "I believe." This was because they were intended to be the statement of the whole Christian community.

The two most famous conciliar creeds from the time were the Symbol of Nicea I, promulgated by the Council of Nicea (325) to refute Arianism and using the philosophical term *homoousios*, "of the same *substance* as the Father," to identify Jesus as divine, and the Nicene-Constantinopolitan Creed promulgated after the Council of Constantinople in 381 and used in Christian worship to this day. The Arian crisis had not been resolved, despite the efforts of the bishops at Nicea, and the term "substance" remained ambiguous. Many other synods were called subsequently in the mid-fourth century and these issued creedal statements purporting to be orthodox, such as the Second Antiochene Creed, which speaks of "God, Three in Person but One in harmony." By the end of the century, moreover, thanks to the Eunomians and Macedonians, the divinity of the Holy Spirit was coming under duress as well. Consequently, all these issues were addressed and to a large extent authoritatively resolved by the first Council of Constantinople. The council's statements vindicated the positions of Athanasius and the three Cappadocian fathers: Basil of Caesarea (d. 379), Gregory Nazianzen (d. ca. 389), and Gregory of Nyssa (d. ca. 394). For the council's profession of faith we are reliant on the Council of Chalcedon (451), which restated it. It contains a strong anti-Arian line in its second article on the Son and has a clear if restrained affirmation of the divinity of the Holy Spirit in its third article. The Nicene-Constantinopolitan Creed became very successful in both East and West as a standard profession of faith. In the East it was used at baptismal liturgies from the sixth century onward and also at Mass. The Western eucharistic liturgy was slower to adopt it. The Council of Toledo III (589) ordered its use before the Lord's Prayer. In Ireland in the ninth century it was sung after the gospel, and this practice spread through England to Gaul and Northern Europe. Eventually this practice was adopted in Rome in the eleventh century. However, by that time the Western addition of *filioque* (the procession of the Holy Spirit "from the Father and the Son") had become a major cause of division and led eventually to the schism between East and West.

Creeds have performed a number of different functions within ecclesial life. They summarize the contents of revelation, act as a norm for interpreting Scripture, have an important catechetical value, and in the liturgy act as a communal expression of belief. In baptism they are a declaration of the individual's faith in the triune God and of his or her adherence to membership in the Christian community. In private prayer they can become a confession of praise and personal trust. Today the creeds also have an ecumenical value, acting as a basis for dialogue and fundamental baptismal communion between churches. But for theology—and this is the point of discussing them here—the creeds act as a norm of inquiry and a source of magisterial doctrine. In other words, in theology the creeds act as a litmus test of orthodoxy and accuracy against which a theologian's writing can be verified.

This normative function of the creeds within theology began from the fourth and fifth centuries onward. However, note should be taken of other and later professions of faith issued by councils of the church, such as the professions of faith of the Council of Toledo IX, the Fourth Lateran Council, and the Council of Lyons I. Other professions have been promulgated at various times to meet various needs, such as Paul VI's Credo of the People of God (1968). Moreover, within both Tridentine and post-conciliar Catholicism, supplemental creedal declarations and oaths of fidelity are often added to the recitation of the creed at the assumption of ministries or when a person is received into full communion.

Many of the churches of the Reformation also felt the need for creedal-type formularies analogous to the historic creeds to secure and express the doctrinal positions of their communities and to guide theological reflection. Such would be the Lutheran Augsburg Confession (1530) and the First and Second Helvetic Confessions of the Calvinist churches (1566). This trend has continued in recent times with the Barmen Declaration (1934) and the Porvoo Declaration (1993). The Greek and Russian churches hold to the Orthodox Confession of 1643.

Finally, note should be taken once again of the normative function of creeds within theology. The historic creeds have authority for theology, and this was recognized early. They are key "monuments" of tradition, media that transmit the essentials of the Christian faith and by which theology can judge itself. Moreover, the creeds have exercised a critical sociopolitical function within the life of the church, helping to ensure orthodoxy. For instance, before the Councils of Nicea and Constantinople there were doubts and doctrinal disputes about the origin of Christ, different interpretations of Scripture, and warring parties championing one position against another. After those councils the church possessed a clear and authoritative statement of faith, with fixed principles for interpreting the Scriptures and for determining eucharistic and ecclesial communion. Today the prestige of the creeds continues to be recognized because of their antiquity and their use over the centuries in the liturgy and in private prayer. On the other hand, their limitations should also be acknowledged. No creed can give a complete statement of Christian doctrine. Moreover, the statements within a creed are open to different interpretations: What does "Son of God" mean? Or belief in "one, holy, catholic, and apostolic church"?

Medieval Theological Methods:
The Quaestio Disputata

If creeds have been important determinants of theological methods since antiquity, the theology of the Middle Ages developed a unique method or approach that helped accelerate a new differentiation within theology. Just as theology in the early church was dominated by doctrinal concerns, so the theology of the medieval period became preoccupied with systematic concerns. This was both reflected and caused by the method of the *quaestio disputata* or "disputed question."

Theology in the Middle Ages developed through the spread of monasticism and the advent of new religious orders and movements from the tenth century onward. Monasteries practiced *lectio divina*, a form of prayerful reflection on a text, be it a book of Scripture or a homily or a commentary of the Fathers. Some scholars wrote commentaries on the Scriptures. Others, as they copied the manuscripts, added a "gloss" to the text, a *glossa* being a word written in the margin or between the lines in order to explain the meaning of a term. Some of these *glossae* were included in subsequent editions. Indeed, two such works became the most important exegetical sources of the Middle Ages: the *Glossa Ordinaria* of the ninth-century German monk Walafrid Strabo (d. 849), made up of lines from the Fathers applied to the individual verses of the Scriptures, and the famous *Glossa Interlineans* of Anselm of Laon (d. 1117), the "Doctor Scholasticus," an interlinear commentary on the whole of the Vulgate. Sometimes the *glossae* were joined together into *catenae* ("chains"), literally chains or collections of the sayings of the Fathers strung together to form a continuous commentary on a book of Scripture. There are numerous examples of such *catenae* in the medieval era, from the time of Alcuin (d. 804) and Rhabanus Maurus (d. 856) to Hugh of St. Victor (d. 1141) and the famous *Catena Aurea* (1263) of Aquinas, a truly monumental collection of patristic sayings on every line of the gospels.

Another medieval theological form was the *florilegium* (lit. a collection of flowers or an anthology), that is, a collection of passages from the Fathers and early writers, usually on a dogmatic or moral theme. A notorious sort of *florilegium* was the *Sic et Non* of Peter Abelard (d. 1142), which as its name ("Yes and No") suggests, listed side by side apparent textual contradictions between the Fathers and the Scriptures, arranged for and against, without determining which opinion was correct. Thus Matthew 5:44 ("Love your enemies and pray for those who persecute you") might be juxtaposed with Matthew 18:6 ("If any of you put a stumbling block before one of these little ones who believe in me, it would be better for you if a great millstone were fastened around your neck and you were drowned in the depth of the sea").

Mention should also be made of an important early medieval theological form, the *sententiae*, which paved the way for the *quaestio*. *Sententiae* were short aphorisms and expositions of a truth of faith. Hugh of St. Victor detailed the approach: first, explain the words; next, expound the literal meaning; finally, fill out the implications and offer an evaluation. The most famous sentences were those of Peter Lombard (d. 1160). Lombard's *Sententiae* (1148–51) ran to four volumes on God One and Three, creation, Christ and redemption, and the sacraments and eschatology.

The *quaestio* evolved in harmony with the university system. In the scholastic period the monastic schools developed into the first universities, whose curriculum began with the *trivium* (grammar, dialectics or logic, and rhetoric) followed by the *quadrivium* (arithmetic, geometry, music, and astronomy). These in turn were followed by the higher study of theology. The study of *sacra doctrina* (the truths of faith taught by the authorities of the past) became distinct from the study of *sacra scriptura* and the work of biblical commentaries. However, the High Middle Ages was a time of great growth in knowledge, with many new ideas and currents of thought flooding Europe, and this paved the way for an ever-increasing specialization in canon law, philosophy, preliminary studies, spirituality, and so on. The scholastic concern was for rational order, coherence, and meaning, with a deeper understanding of the Christian faith and how it was structured. There was also the issue of how the many and varied truths of the Christian faith fit together, given that the sources sometimes appeared to be full of contradictions and conflicts.

Significantly, this led to a new pedagogical method for doing theology: the *quaestio disputata* or academic disputation. Pupils or others put disputed issues to the teacher in the form of a question for him to be resolved and answered in light of the traditional sources and authorities. The

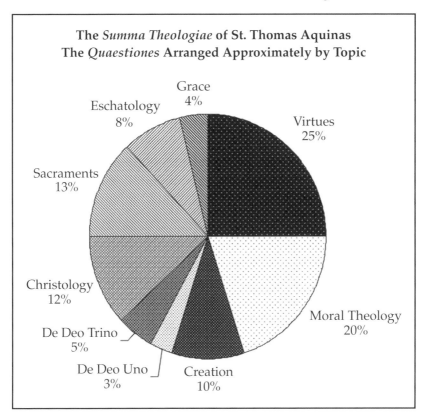

The *Summa Theologiae* of St. Thomas Aquinas
The *Quaestiones* Arranged Approximately by Topic

Figure 8

quaestio approach gave rise to the great compendia or *Summa* of theology, philosophy, and canon law, such as the *Summa Aurea* of William of Auxerre (d. 1231), one of the first theological works to be influenced by the recovered Aristotelian philosophy. Another was the *Summa Universae Theologiae* of the English-born Alexander Hales (d. 1245), which cites a triple series of authorities—those saying yes, those saying no, and then the reconciliation or judgment—from the Bible, the Fathers, Greek, Latin, and Arabic poets and philosophers, as well as later theologians. A further example was the two-volume *Summa Theologiae* of the German Dominican, Albert the Great (d. 1280). These handbooks came to replace *sententiae* in teaching theology. The most famous were, of course, those of Aquinas: the *Summa Contra Gentiles* (1264), thought to have been written originally for missionary use, and the *Summa Theologiae* (1274).

It is interesting to note the concerns the *quaestiones* dealt with (see figure 8). A crudely simplistic glance at Aquinas's questions in his *Summa*

Theologiae reveals the theocentric worldview of the time, with its focus on living a virtuous life in the present world with the hope of heaven. Thus 70 percent of the questions in the *Summa Theologiae* regard moral theology, the virtues, grace, eschatology, and the sacraments; 18 percent have to do with dogmatic theology, and 12 percent with Christology.

Catechisms and the Reformation

In the later Middle Ages, as already noted, theology, spirituality, and philosophy became distinct. This was in part because of the great debates of the time: in philosophy, principally the discussion of Platonism versus Aristotelianism or the nominalism-realism dispute over universals. The new movements in spirituality included the *devotio moderna*, which began under Geert Groote (d. 1384) in the Netherlands and spread across Europe. It was a call to biblical simplicity, to a personal relationship with Christ—particularly Christ in his suffering, passion, and death on the cross—and to an interior life based on the Eucharist rather than on communal devotions and formal practices. The *devotio moderna* was successful principally among the laity and gave rise to the "Beguine" movement and to a number of new religious orders. Its classic text was *The Imitation of Christ* (1418) by Thomas à Kempis (d. 1471). Mention should also be made here of some of the other great saints and spiritual writers of the times such as Meister Eckhart (d. 1327), Johannes Tauler (d. 1361), Blessed Henry Suso (d. 1366), and the English mystic Julian of Norwich (d. ca. 1416).

The medieval period was eventually overlaid by the Renaissance and the religious Reformation. The late fifteenth and early sixteenth centuries, characterized by increasing decadence within the church, also saw a revival of the study of Greek and Hebrew, together with a renewed interest in classical literature. Petrarch (Francesco Petrarca, d. 1374), the so-called father of humanism, was one of the authors of this renaissance of learning. There was also a resurgence of interest in the Bible, with new methods of scholarship based on a return to the sources and the study of the texts in their original languages. Prototypical here was Desiderius Erasmus (d. 1536), one-time Lady Margaret Professor of Divinity at Cambridge, who taught himself Greek and Hebrew. He published in 1516 the *Novum Testamentum omne, diligenter ab Erasmo Rot. Recognitum et Emendatum*, later known as the *Textus Receptus*, the first published Greek New Testament, incorporating a new Latin translation, some brief exegetical points, and an impassioned exhortation encouraging study of the Bible.

By the mid-sixteenth century all theology began to adopt an increasingly polemical stance amid the challenges of the Reformation, aided by advances in printing technology. One of the new theological forms that emerged from this period was the catechism, a summary or manual of doctrine, often in the form of questions followed by answers to be memorized. Catechisms and tracts were first published by the Reformers, notably Martin Luther, who commissioned a *Large Catechism* (1529) with five parts (the Ten Commandments, the Apostles' Creed, the Lord's Prayer, baptism, and the Sacrament of the Altar) addressed to the clergy to help them instruct the faithful, and a *Small Catechism* (1529) for children. John Calvin (d. 1564) produced the *Geneva Catechism* (1542, revised in 1545 and 1560), which he organized around the topics of faith, law, prayer, and the sacraments. Mention should be made of the 1548 Catechism of Thomas Cranmer (d. 1556), which in modified form was incorporated into the 1549, 1552, and 1559 versions of the *Book of Common Prayer*.

These Protestant and Anglican catechisms were so successful that many were leaving the Catholic Church, and so, in 1555, the German Jesuit Peter Canisius (d. 1597) produced a catechism for popular use among Roman Catholics. It was eventually translated into many languages and underwent innumerable subsequent editions. However, at the suggestion of Charles Borromeo (d. 1584), the Council of Trent commissioned its own catechism, the *Roman Catechism* or *Catechism of the Council of Trent* (1566), addressed to pastoral clergy to assist them in instructing the faithful. This catechism, which enjoyed unique authority until the publication of the *Catechism of the Catholic Church* in 1992, contained four sections: the Apostles' Creed, the sacraments, the Ten Commandments, and prayer.

For theology, catechisms as such do not have the authority of the creeds or of papal and conciliar definitions. They are designed, however, to "fill out" the creeds and to disseminate doctrine within the everyday life of the church. They have a normative function similar to the creeds and possess prestige as an exposition of doctrine, as the debates surrounding the publication of the 1992 *Catechism of the Catholic Church* showed.

Thesis Theology and Neoscholasticism

A new form of theology that emerged around the time of the Council of Trent would eventually characterize all Catholic theology in the period from the Enlightenment to Vatican II, namely, thesis theology, the use of proof texts, originally pioneered by the Spanish Dominican Melchior Cano (d. 1560). In his posthumously published *De Locis Theologicis* (1562), Cano sought to free dogmatic theology from the vain disputes of this or that school of thought by recalling theology to its sources and by developing a systematic presentation of the orthodox faith according to a uniform and coordinated method. The *De Locis* was about the ten *loci* or sources of theology: Scripture, oral tradition, the church itself, the councils of the church, the Fathers of the church, the Roman pontiff, the scholastic theologians, natural reason, the authority of philosophers, and the authority of history. Subsequent theologians took up these *loci* and used them in order to defend disputed points of doctrine by appealing to this or that source or authority. Initially the defense was against the challenge of the Reformers and mainly concerned the nature of the church and the sacraments, but with the Enlightenment and the advent of modernity, thesis theology sought to defend the faith from all sorts of challenges raised by the modern era. The purpose was to give an easy and sound transmission of the deposit of faith for the use of clergy and religious.

A mid-twentieth-century version of this kind of thesis theology can be seen in the remarkable *Fundamentals of Catholic Dogma* (1952) by Ludwig Ott, a comprehensive survey of all the principal doctrines the church was said to teach. Ott stated and "proved" each thesis, identifying its status and its source in Scripture, in councils and papal pronouncements, as well as in the writings of the Fathers and the chief theologians. Its doctrinal value was also indicated according to an ascending scale from *opinio* to *de fide definita*. Thesis theology and neoscholastic theology in general gave considerable attention to these "Theological Notes," which expressed the value and grade of certainty attached to magisterial pronouncements. By these notes neoscholastic theology, at least in theory, conceded that not all the teachings of the church were taught irrevocably and with the same solemn authority. For instance, the thesis "With Christ and the apostles, general revelation ended" had, according to Ott, the value *sententia certa* attached in brackets. Typical notes are those outlined in figure 9.

It is illuminating to compare the theological method used by thesis theology with that of Aquinas. Aquinas poses a question to which the answer is going to be either yes or no (see figure 10). He begins with the *videtur quod non* ("it seems not"), that is, the arguments in the various sources and authorities against the answer to be given, with the main disputed issues. Then, in the *sed contra* ("but on the other hand"), Thomas states the answer, his own judgment, followed by an explanation (*respondeo*: lit. "I respond") of why he gave this or that answer, together with the arguments that back up his position. Finally, he gives answers (*responsa*) to the initial objections and counterpositions.

Theological Notes

de fide definita	truths immediately revealed by God or taught solemnly by the church, often in the form of a dogma
sententia fidei proxima	other teachings proximate to faith and regarded by theologians as truths of revelation even though not defined solemnly
sententia communis	a common teaching of the church not solemnly defined but held by most theologians
sententia probabilis, sententia probabilior, sententia bene fundata	(in decreasing order) theological opinions of varying degrees of certainty
sententia pia	a pious opinion
opinio tolerata	a tolerated opinion

Figure 9

Significantly, in contrast to Aquinas's way of beginning with a *quaestio*, thesis theology begins with an answer—that is, a thesis it then proceeds to justify by an appeal to the various authorities and sources (see figure 11). The inquiry of the *quaestio* has been replaced by the pedagogy of the thesis (Lonergan). Thus in a section on the angels the first thesis is justified from Scripture alone whereas the second, which we are told is *de fide*, is justified by an appeal to the liturgy, the fact that there is a feast day in honor of the Guardian Angels, and also by an appeal to Scripture and to patristic literature.

Thesis theology had the evident advantage of presenting a strong and clear defense of Catholic doctrine with an accent on the certitudes of faith, their presuppositions, and their consequences, easily grasped by pastor and faithful alike. Its presentation of the range of Catholic theology could be put to good catechetical and apologetic use. Moreover, it corresponded in some respects to an innate *intellectus fidei* that seeks to justify belief or doctrinal claims by an appeal to the sources in Scripture, tradition, and magisterium. Yet its tight methodology disguised some fundamental flaws. In the first place, apart from the creeds and the solemn dogmatic statements of the popes and councils, there has never been in the church a generally agreed list of doctrinal theses with their values. Not even the universally respected reference work *Enchiridion symbolorum definitionum et declarationum de rebus fidei et morum* of Heinrich Denzinger (d. 1883) and Adolf Schönmetzer, first published in 1854 with

AQUINAS: THE METHOD OF THE *QUAESTIO*
as Illustrated by the First Question of the *Summa Theologiae*

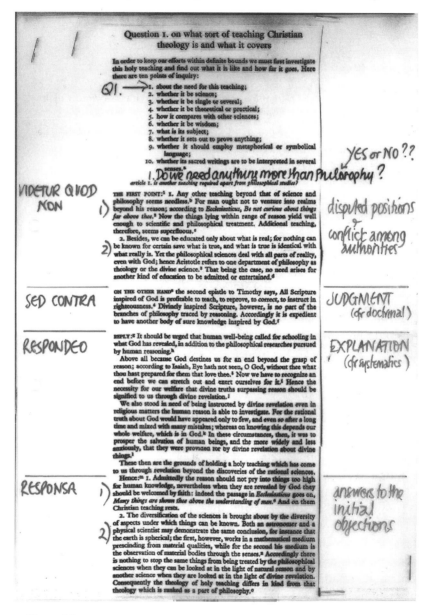

Figure 10

EXAMPLE OF THESIS THEOLOGY
Excerpt from Ludwig Ott's, *The Fundamentals of Catholic Dogma*

120   God the Creator

The belief of Origen and of many of his followers (St. Gregory of Nyssa, Didymus of Alexandria, Evagrius Ponticus) concerning the restoration of all things (ἀποκατάστασις πάντων ; cf Act 13, 21), according to which the damned angels and men, after a long period of purification, will be re-established in grace and will return to God, was rejected at a Synod of Constantinople (543) as heretical. D 211 ; cf. D 429.

§ 30. The Efficacy of the Good Angels

1. Relation to God

The primary task of the good angels is the glorification and the service of God. (*Sent. certa.*)

Holy Writ adjures the angels to praise God and attests that they glorify God by their praise. Cf. Ps. 102, 20 et seq. : " Bless the Lord all ye his angels ! " Cf. Ps. 148, 2 ; Dn. 3, 58 ; Is. 6, 3 ; Apoc. 4, 8 ; 5, 11 et seq. ; Hebr. 1, 6. God is served as well as praised. As ambassadors of God the angels transmit revelations and directions to mankind. Cf. Luke 1, 11 et seq. ; 1, 26 et seq. ; Mt. 1, 20 et seq. ; Luke 2, 9 et seq. ; Mt. 2, 13. 19 et seq. ; Acts 5, 19 et seq. ; 8, 26 ; 10, 3 et seq. ; 12, 7 et seq.

2. Relation to Man

a) The secondary task of the good angels is the protection of men and care for their salvation. (*De fide on the ground of general teaching.*)

Since the 16th century the Church celebrates a feast in honour of the guardian angels. The Roman Catechism (IV, 9, 4) teaches : " By God's Providence the task is given to the angels of protecting the human race and individual human beings, so that they may not suffer any serious harm whatever."

Holy Writ testifies that all the angels are in the service of mankind. Hebr. 1, 14 : " Are they not all ministering angels, sent to minister for them who shall receive the inheritance of salvation ? " Ps. 90, 11 et seq., describes the care of the angels for the just. Cf. Gn. 24, 7 ; Ex. 23, 20 23 ; Ps. 33, 8 ; Jdt. 13, 20 ; Tob. 5, 27 ; Dn. 3, 49 ; 6, 22.

According to Origen (De princ. I Praed. 10) it is " a constituent part of the doctrinal promulgation of the Church that there are angels of God and benevolent powers, which serve Him, in order to complete the salvation of mankind." Cf. Origen, contra Celsum, VIII 34.

b) Every one of the faithful has his own special guardian angel from baptism. (*Sent. certa.*)

According to the general teaching of the theologians, however, not only every baptised person, but every human being, including unbelievers, has his own special guardian angel from his birth. This view is biblically founded on the words of Our Lord. Mt. 18. 10 : " See that you do not despise one of

Figure 11

its lists of numbers beginning "DS" alongside the lines and paragraphs of magisterial pronouncements, nor the similar collection in English translation, *The Christian Faith in the Doctrinal Documents of the Catholic Church* (latest edition 2001), edited by Jacques Dupuis, are official collections as such. Contrary to the impression given, everything in thesis theology, as in these and other reference works, depends entirely on the genius and prestige of the theologian selecting and presenting the theses and their accompanying material.

Thesis theology was almost completely inadequate for dealing with modern critical and historical scholarship. It treated its source texts in a precritical, ahistorical fashion, taking the sayings of Scripture and the Fathers out of context or failing to take into account their original meanings. It denied the development of doctrine. Modern historical scholarship and religious studies have now stripped this approach of many of its sources or at least, thanks to the new methods of historical inquiry, revised their meaning. Moreover, the concerns of thesis theology were driven fundamentally by the needs of Reformation polemics, designed to show that the Roman Catholic Church was the one, true church. Today, by contrast, theology has adopted a more irenic and ecumenical, indeed, interreligious approach. Further, the deductive method and appeal to authority of thesis theology was highly contestable, as was the manner whereby it correlated the respective roles of the magisterium, theologians, and the faithful.

Thesis theology presumed that the questions that lay behind the theses were actually the questions people wanted to ask. In reality, the questions embedded in the theses were those needed to communicate an overview of the Catholic faith and to defend that faith, yet these may not have been the real-life, existential questions people wished to have answered. In this way such a theology ran the risk of making the Christian faith irrelevant to modern living. Indeed, according to Lonergan thesis theology, popular in Catholic seminaries and universities from the eighteenth century onward, was a defensive reaction not only against the Reformers but also more generally against modernity. By it, he said, Catholic theology "retreated into a dogmatic corner." By this he meant that Catholic theology accented the truths of faith, with a strong emphasis on dogma, at the very time when the real need was for intelligibility and understanding, for a grasp of the meaning and relevance of the Christian faith and belief in God in a secular and pluralist world.

One of the strengths of neoscholastic theology, it might be argued, was its division of the theological enterprise into clearly defined departments—e.g., apologetics, dogma, moral theology, spirituality, liturgy, and patristics—with their highly sophisticated treatises. These would include revelation, ecclesiology, *De Deo Uno, De Deo Trino*, creation, eschatology, grace, the virtues, and so on. Neoscholasticism also made a clear distinction between "judgment" and "understanding or interpretation," a distinction that gave rise to positive or historical theology on the one hand and speculative and systematic theology on the other. These two functions, which would be undertaken by the same theologian in the same treatise, were always to be seen as complementary, even if—in seminaries at least—doctrinal theology gained the upper hand.

Thus the treatise on, say, the sacrament of baptism would begin with a dogmatic thesis on one or other aspect of the sacrament. The positive moment would justify that thesis by appeal to the sources in Scripture (the data given in the Old, then the New, Testaments), the Fathers, the statements of the popes, councils, and other magisterium, the witness of the liturgy, and the sayings of the doctors and theologians, and in this way would seek to establish the truth of faith on this or that aspect of the sacrament of baptism. The aim of positive theology was to identify and define the truth Christ had revealed, as expressed in Scripture and tradition. Then, in a second phase, the theologian would embark on a systematic moment, seeking to understand and explore further this doctrine, its intelligibility, and its meaning, the objections to it, the disputed issues involved, together with any speculative questions to be raised. The aim of speculative theology was the *intellectus fidei* ("understanding of the faith"), an attempt to penetrate the mystery by faith-filled reason, to understand, and to systematize.

Finally, mention must be made of the manner in which neoscholasticism perceived the relationship of theologians to the church, especially to church authority. In the Middle Ages the term "magisterium" (Lat. *magister*, "teacher") implied an element of authority, as in *minus* "less" and *magis* "more," and thus signified one with authority, the mastery of one who teaches. This authority was symbolized by the chair (*cathedra*), as today when people speak of a chair in a university or the chair of a committee or the bishop's chair in the cathedral. Aquinas distinguished two kinds of magisterium (*In IV Sent*, 19.2.2, q.3, sol.2, ad 4): the *magisterium cathedrae pastoralis* (the authority of the pastoral chair, i.e., of the bishop) and the *magisterium cathedrae magistralis* (the professional chair of the theologian). The bishop's authority was based on ordination, on being a successor to the apostles; the theologian's, on a knowledge of theology, on being an expert with competence and authority within the field. In the Middle Ages many of the theological disputes that racked the church were given to theologians to settle, the bishops then following the best advice given. In this way theologians played a critical role, even at the Council of Trent. Recently in the light of this some have spoken of twin or parallel magisteria in the church, that of the hierarchy and that of theologians. Yet historically this has never meant that theologians and bishops exercised equal or the same authority. Aquinas, for example, insisted that bishops had the ultimate right to judge in a doctrinal dispute, even if the argumentation and matter in general were left to theologians. Moreover, since Vatican I magisterium has come to mean exclusively the teaching authority of the church (*Dei Filius* 3011), that is, the authority of the pope (*Pastor Aeternus*, DS 3065) and the bishops (*Lumen Gentium* 25) and those institutions directly responsible to them such as the CDF, which have the divinely mandated authority to give a definitive, juridically binding interpretation.

The relationship between theologians and the magisterium became difficult with the onset of modernity, and particularly in the nineteenth and twentieth centuries with the challenges of modernism. Tridentine Catholicism had a strongly pyramidal character with an increasingly authoritarian edge. Theology became increasingly a deductive rather than an investigative science, static not dynamic, abstract not particular, defensive rather than open. Consequently, neoscholasticism tended to portray theologians as the servants of the magisterium, the pope and bishops alone having the mission to teach, with theologians having the task of explanation. In his 1950 encyclical *Humani Generis*, Pius XII, citing Pius IX's *Inter gravissimas* (1870), put it like this:

> It is for [the theologian] to show how the doctrine of the teaching authority of the Church is contained in Scripture and in the sacred Tradition, whether explicitly or implicitly. (Pius XII, *Humani Generis*, DS 3886/ND 859)

This view derived in part from the ecclesiology of Robert Bellarmine, who envisaged the church as made up of two parts: the *ecclesia docens*, the teaching church, formed of the pope and bishops divinely mandated to teach the truth of Christ, and the *ecclesia discens*, the learning and listening church, formed of all the other members, including theologians. Thus the pope and, to a lesser extent, the bishops were the custodians of the deposit of revelation and the truths of faith, with the theologians delegated by them to explain those truths to the rest. Richard Gaillardetz (b. 1958), in his *By What Authority? A Primer on Scripture, the Magisterium, and the Sense of the Faithful* (2003), depicts this model as in figure 12.

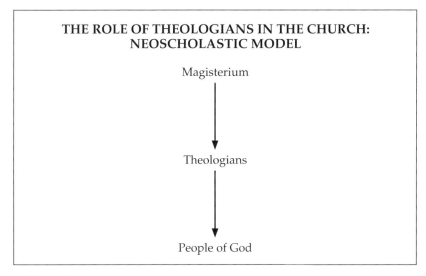

Figure 12

Vatican II and the Crisis of Method

The renewal of ecclesiology began in earnest with the *Nouvelle Théolo-gie*, although it was foreshadowed in the nineteenth century by Newman and by the Tübingen School. Thus in his 1877 *Preface to the Via Media*, Newman spoke of three offices within the church, the faithful (formed of priests and laity), the theologians, and the hierarchy of pope and bishops. He associated these offices with Christ as priest, prophet, and shepherd and outlined how they led to the church's triple function of worship, teaching, and governance with their respective concerns for holiness, truth, and unity. The renewed ecclesiology, resulting from a return to the sources in Scripture and the Fathers together with a richer theology of revelation, in which revelation was seen less as a collection of propositional truths and more as an encounter with the person of Christ, shifted toward a less pyramidal structure. This brought about a new vision of the relationship of bishops and theologians as suggested in the practice of Vatican II, which many theologians attended as *periti* and theological advisers. However, in the period after the council, par-ticularly after the publication of Paul VI's *Humanae Vitae*, various high-profile disputes between the Vatican and individual theologians attracted mass media attention, with a popular perception that the magisterium was the last vestige of tradition and authoritarianism. Indeed, at the Extraordinary Synod of 1985, called to commemorate the twentieth anniversary of Vatican II, a need was expressed for the clarification of the status of theologians within the church and their relationship to the magisterium. This was the background to the remarkable CDF *Instruction on the Ecclesial Vocation of the Theologian* (1990), which sought to create a new framework for the relationship between the magisterium, theologians, and the church.

The title of the *Instruction* in itself was noteworthy, a statement that theologians were meant to be first and foremost members of the church hierarchically constituted and that theology was a vocation, a God-given call and gift of the Holy Spirit for the service of the people of God (6). The *Instruction* began with a discussion about truth: that truth is a gift in the person of Christ, and that by abiding in the truth that is Christ human beings can find liberation from the slavery of error and darkness. Both the magisterium and theologians, each in their own way, one a hierarchical gift to the church, the other a charismatic gift, were at the service of the truth (2-5). The magisterium had the mandate of safeguarding the deposit of faith, assisted by the charism of infallibility (13-20), and so relations between theology and the magisterium should be collaborative (21-31), theologians acknowledging the legitimate authority of the magisterium, the magisterium acknowledging that for the exercise of its authority it requires the collaboration of theologians. Both the magisterium and theology have the same goal, truth (21), and so relations should be governed by a concern for truth and charity (26), theologians presenting their conclusions tentatively (27) while making known to pastors any difficulties (30).

The *Instruction* therefore situates theology and the magisterium within the People of God as a whole, proposing in effect a triangular relationship among the faithful, theology, and the magisterium, all together exploring the Word of God (see figure 13).

This seems to be in marked contrast to the previous neoscholastic model. On the other hand, some have commented that while the *Instruction* said much about the duties of theologians, it said little on the corresponding duties of the magisterium toward theology. Surely, they said, the magisterium has responsibilities, such as eschewing anti-intellectualism, utilizing the gifts of theologians, avoiding "police-state tactics" or overly zealous interventions without trying to understand a theologian's work or allowing theology an opportunity to police itself? Indeed, do not bishops have a duty to teach the truth, to present official teaching clearly and attractively and, rather than opting for safety by keeping silent, to guide the faithful on controversial issues?

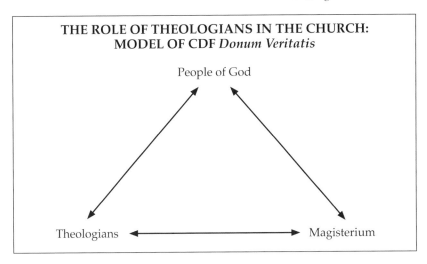

Figure 13

One other feature of the CDF *Instruction* deserves mention. In the period after Vatican II, "Theological Notes" fell into disuse amid the theological upheavals of the times. However, the new phenomenon of widespread dissent then appeared—with, on the one hand, the challenge of "dogmatic positivism" (the idea that the only doctrines to be believed are those the church has solemnly defined) and, on the other, the charge of "creeping infallibilism" (the assertion that everything the church states is infallibly expressed). This led to much discussion about the weight of authority involved in such magisterial teaching as that of *Humanae Vitae*. The 1990 CDF *Instruction* was the first magisterial document ever to deal with this. Paragraphs 23 and 24 outlined four types of magisterial teaching, with the responses due, and the new position, which required certain amendments to both the *Code of Canon Law* and the *Code of Canons of the Eastern Churches*, was filled out further in a *motu proprio* from John Paul II, *Ad Tuendam Fidem* (1998) and in the doctrinal commentary accompanying it from the CDF. The four types of doctrine and the appropriate responses can be summarized as outlined in figure 14.

The first two categories of doctrine were interrelated, although as the American Jesuit Francis Sullivan pointed out in his *Creative Fidelity: Weighing and Interpreting Documents of the Magisterium* (1996), the parameters of the second category can be somewhat ill-defined and elusive when applied to the pronouncements of the ordinary magisterium. Most teaching would belong to the third category, namely, doctrines connected with

CATEGORIES OF DOCTRINE AND FAITH RESPONSE Cf. CDF *Donum Veritatis*	
Church Teaching	**Faith Response**
Revealed truths and solemn definitions	Assent of faith
Definitive truths of faith	Firm acceptance
Ordinary authoritative teaching	Submission of intellect and will
Prudential decisions	Conscientious obedience

Figure 14

revelation and filling out the implications of revelation for Christian living in new situations and contexts, but not yet irreversibly defined or definitively proposed. In paragraph 24 the *Instruction* spoke of a fourth category of judgments and decisions made from time to time on questions that were still under discussion and that might involve contingent or conjectural elements. The clarification the *Instruction* offered in outlining these four grades of magisterial teaching was on the whole well received at the time, although the "new" gradations are rarely referred to in practice either by theologians or, perhaps surprisingly, by the CDF itself. If anything, certain subsequent magisterial pronouncements became the focus of intense debate precisely over the doctrinal value of their statements. Such was the Apostolic Letter of John Paul II, *Ordinatio Sacerdotalis* (1994), on reserving priestly ordination to men alone. This latter required a *Responsum ad dubium* from the CDF in 1995 and an explanatory letter.

More generally, Vatican II constituted for Catholic theology a watershed, the moment when it began to take seriously the modern world, modern science, and modern critical scholarship, with in most cases an openness to engagement and dialogue with that world. Yet at the same time the demise of a unitary philosophy (Thomism and the classical tradition) led to a new pluralism, with individualist approaches, increased specialization, and a certain amount of polarization. For much of its history Catholic theology has been absorbed in ensuring an orthodox communication of church doctrine both within the church and without. Today, however, it could be argued that the very openness of theology has led it to pay less attention to doctrine and more to simple understanding, interpretation, and exploration. Many new questions have arisen and require an answer, thanks in part to the enormous amount of new data discovered by critical scholarship investigating the sources such as the Bible and church history. This has weakened the dogmatic component within Catholic theology, yet it has strengthened and energized systematic interests.

Each individual theologian now chooses his or her own approach and theological method, approaching a given topic according to her or his own *a priori* questions and concerns. This has resulted in rampant and often conflictual pluralism with manifold fragmentations, collisions, and often false dichotomies. Unsurprisingly, there have been collisions between the Vatican and theologians. More generally, a rift has opened between critical-academic Catholic theology and pastoral-systematic Catholic theology. Thus academic theology is studied and taught in universities by highly qualified laymen and laywomen, whereas seminary theology is associated with the pastoral reality of the worshiping community, usually the responsibility of the clergy. In the 1980s and 1990s new ecclesial movements emerged, often among younger believers, that savored of fundamentalism and espoused an older-style or reactionary dogmatism, and these were often spurned by those who saw themselves as the true guardians of the progressive "spirit" of Vatican II. The insights of biblical scholarship appear to be unevenly related to doctrine or to threaten its foundations. The pastoral reality of the church at the parish level is often marked by dislocations between theory and practice (as in regard to the blessing of invalid marriages), between personal conviction and ecclesiastical law (as with respect to the reception of communion by those in irregular situations), and between the spiritual and the academic, so that the study of the Word of God appears dry and intellectualist, not associated realistically with the life of personal prayer and devotion.

All these factors and others, it could be argued, have made the issue of theological method critically important in the twenty-first century if the gains of modern theology on the one hand and the historic unity of faith on the other are to be preserved and correlated. The need is universally felt for a greater unity amid the fragmentation of modern theology: the correlation of biblical exegesis with church doctrine, theological theory with pastoral praxis, and a greater unity between theology as a whole and other modern disciplines and domains of knowledge, so that the Catholic tradition can enter into a critical yet mutually enriching conversation with contemporary culture. Bernard Lonergan once observed that the contemporary situation was not unlike that faced by Aquinas in the thirteenth century when new insights from Aristotle, science, and the Arabic world were flooding medieval Europe. Aquinas's achievement was to synthesize the new with the old, and, Lonergan argued, this is today's task too:

> To follow Aquinas today is not to repeat Aquinas today, but to do for the twentieth century what Aquinas did for the thirteenth. As Aquinas baptised key elements in Greek and Arabic culture, so the contemporary catholic philosopher and/or theologian has to effect a baptism of key elements in modern culture. (Bernard Lonergan, "Theology and Man's Future," *A Second Collection*, 138)

2. Some Current Styles of Theology

We conclude with some observations on current theological styles and methods. A method is a device or approach for getting a job done: boiling an egg, repairing a car, finding a book in the library, and so on. Ordinarily, method is not a topic of conversation except when learning a new one or when someone asks how we managed to do X or Y. To grasp what might be meant by method in theology, we could take the example of a line from Scripture and ask what its meaning is. For instance, what is the meaning of John 10:16 ("I have other sheep that do not belong to this fold. I must bring them also, and they will listen to my voice. So there will be one flock, one shepherd")? Method here is how we go about answering that type of question: the order of procedure, the sources that need to be consulted, the types of exegesis and hermeneutics to be used, the historical disputes involved, the traditional ecclesial and doctrinal parameters, the process of making and verifying a correct judgment, the implications of the answer for other disciplines and fields of inquiry, and the pastoral applications.

Today's growing preoccupation with theological method is no doubt the product of a long crisis, or series of crises, in Western thought dating back to the breakup of the great medieval syntheses and the consequent fragmentations and pluralisms it caused. Today there is a variety of theological methods in use, depending largely on the task at hand and the context or destination the theologian wishes to communicate with. Moreover, in terms of studying and conducting theology there are numerous options.

A good method might be the simple one of selecting a suitable *magister* or *magistra*, an outstanding theologian to follow, and then, as an apprentice, learning from her or him how to do theology.

The Roman method of theologizing retains a good deal of prestige. Its hallmark is the differentiation of positive from speculative theology. It elaborates a history of doctrine by tracing the development of a position through the sources (from the Old to the New Testament, the Fathers, the liturgy, the statements of popes and councils, down to the present) and then offers a systematic theology that deals with the interpretation of the doctrine and the speculative questions arising.

The historical approach is another possibility; it leads to a hermeneutics or critical commentary that interprets the context of the past in order to determine what is applicable to present circumstances. Alternatively, a discursive, narrative, or literary appeal to personal experience might be the way forward. This is favored by spiritual writers and those theologians who desire to recover "story" as used by Christ in the gospels.

Again, one could take a contextual approach in which attention is given to the theological meaning and value of the cultural context in which the Christian life has to be lived.

This section will focus on the types or styles of theology currently to be found within Roman Catholic thought. To simplify matters, canon law, philosophy, and spirituality—the literature specifically related to prayer and personal development—will be omitted in favor of the more strictly theological. Of the many styles presently to be found within theology, four are selected here for consideration. These are readily recognizable: (1) the doctrinal-catechetical, (2) the critical-historical, (3) the contextual-experiential, and (4) the transcendental. These styles will be examined, compared, and contrasted. Attention will be given to the philosophical commitments that underpin them and create trajectories of thought their practitioners find fruitful for their theology. The aim is to help readers identify these styles in order thereby to reach a more critical assessment of the contemporary situation.

The first two styles (the doctrinal-catechetical and critical-historical) are forms of theology that start from the side of the object of theology and its sources, whereas the second two (the contextual-experiential and the transcendental) start from the subject, that is, from human persons and their experience or from the culture and context in which theology is being done. The first two could be said to be loosely concerned with metaphysical issues. They are within the "wisdom" tradition of theology, *fides quaerens intellectum*. The second two are generally concerned with epistemological issues and, particularly in the third style, are oriented toward action and transformation. These styles understand theology as *fides quaerens actionem*.

An important proviso, however, is necessary. Few theologians fit easily within categories, not even within the models or styles described here. Theologians often write in different styles depending on the task at hand, and even then, within the same work, adopt a variety of methods. Some are more self-conscious than others about the methods they use. Lonergan warns us that the use of models and ideal types has limits. Unless attentively, intelligently, reasonably, and responsibly devised and applied, they become defective and act as "anti-comprehension machines," massively distorting the data. Readers, because they are unable to see the situation accurately, thus misunderstand and misjudge it. A common instance of this is the use of labels derived from political categories. Theologies and theologians are frequently pigeonholed as left wing or right wing, progressive or conservative, liberal or traditional. In fact, much of theology itself as well as the present situation is more complex than this, even if some thinkers are more avowedly concerned with preserving the past than others who wish to change the present. Crude labels can thus impugn theological discourse by distorting the data, clouding the issues, misjudging the situation, and preventing informed discussion. Another issue connected with this is the use of the term "orthodox," which is a statement about right worship and the truth. Being orthodox is often confusedly associated with traditionalism, as if it were not possible to be orthodox and progressive. In fact, orthodoxy, that which is the truth, is the opposite of heterodoxy, that which is not the truth, and truth, within the tradition, is invariably something of a broad river. This is why the category of orthodoxy is distinct from attitudes taken toward it, such as conservativism or progressivism.

The Doctrinal-Catechetical Style

The first style to be considered here, the doctrinal-catechetical, is easily the most widespread and well known. To most members of the church it is barely noticeable as a theological style but is the only kind of theology they know. This style is the usual, "official" teaching-type theology in use throughout the church and adapted to circumstances and conditions. It is familiar to all Roman Catholics from its use in doctrinal, catechetical, and apologetic materials, the *Catechism of the Catholic Church*, prayer books, liturgical books, the documents of Vatican II, papal and Vatican instructions, official church statements, and in the preaching, teaching, and exhortations of pastors. It is a form of theologizing concerned with expounding, explaining, and communicating the doctrine, life, and worship of the church in order to nourish faith, to lead to a deeper relationship with God, to prompt conversion, to insert listeners more deeply into the paschal mystery, to inform and expand one's understanding of the meaning of the Gospel, to correct erroneous practices and misunderstandings, and generally to insert its recipients more deeply into the life of Christ and the church. This style, therefore, focuses on the sources of faith in the Scriptures and in tradition, in the liturgy, in the patristic corpus, in the creeds and declarations of church councils and synods, in the pronouncements of the popes, in the great medieval authorities, especially Augustine and Aquinas, and in the life, witness, and writings of the saints.

Doctrinal-catechetical theology generally adopts a classical from-above trajectory. It starts with God's self-revelation in Jesus Christ and the transmission of that revelation historically and authoritatively through the church. It tends to be methodical, laying out its subject matter in concentric circles from the ground of faith, the mystery of Christ in a Trinitarian perspective. It may tackle challenges put to the tradition by heretics and controversialists, but its primary purpose is not so much to argue and speculate as to catechize and instruct. It is the direct descendant of the neoscholastic approaches discussed earlier, even if today somewhat chastened by the results of modern biblical and historical scholarship and thus on occasion tending to sound a more restrained note.

Sometimes a "history of doctrine" approach is adopted. This can be seen, for instance, in the Congregation for Divine Worship and the Discipline of the Sacraments' *Directory on Popular Piety and the Liturgy* (2002). After defining what is meant by popular piety and how it relates to the church's public liturgy, the document adopts a historical perspective. It explores features of popular devotion through the ages before looking at the teaching of the church relating to liturgy and piety in order to derive some evaluative theological principles. These principles are then applied to a survey of the current state of the church's devotional life. The second part of the document then lays out guidelines about the liturgical year, devotion to Mary and the saints, intercession for the dead, and shrines and pilgrimages. This historical type of approach, however, is not, as in the next theological style, a "critical" or selective history but rather a demonstration of how current faith and doctrine, liturgy and practice have developed in a continuous line that stretches back to the church of the New Testament era. Doctrinal-catechetical theology in this respect is much akin to the classical method of the "Roman school." Indeed, its presupposition is that today's outcome is what was logically implied in the beginning or was actually present there, despite the occasional variation, and that the present situation is in direct continuity with everything that went before, even if today some aspects need to be amended or renewed.

Another route typically taken by doctrinal-catechetical theology is a "topical" approach. This can be seen in the CDF *Doctrinal Note on Some Aspects of Evangelization* (2007). This relatively brief document begins with the roots of mission and evangelization in the life of Christ and the sending of the apostles. It then applies its understanding to current issues (anthropological, ecclesial, and ecumenical) having to do with evangelization today. Here the approach is not so much historical as the exposition of a thesis. The subject matter to be discussed is first contextualized within church doctrine as a whole, beginning with the words and actions of Christ in Scripture and the teaching and practice of the early church. Then doctrinal, liturgical, or disciplinary matters, particularly those that are perceived as being neglected or in need of recovery, are discussed with reference to previous magisterial teaching and documents. Changes and developments are proposed, and the whole concludes with practical applications and disciplinary norms. In other words, the topic has been comprehensively covered.

The chief purpose of the doctrinal-catechetical style of theology is to teach authoritatively and to expound with clarity the truths of faith, to bring about conformity in behavior and practice, and ultimately to prompt believers to prayer and conversion. It seeks to defend the tradition from its adversaries, to promote unity within the church, and to ensure right belief and practice. It seeks to lead worshipers to prayer and devotion. It is not always gladly received. Some of the declarations and notifications issued by the CDF have been controversial, for example, *Dominus Iesus,* On the Unicity and Salvific Universality of Jesus Christ and the Church (2000), and the warnings about the theological writings of Roger Haight, Jon Sobrino, and Peter Phan (in 2004, 2006, and 2007). Such perceived counterpositions are dealt with, it is said, in order to correct aberrant practices, to strengthen and build up the faith of the listeners, and to equip them with tools and resources for explaining their faith to others.

As a style this kind of theology is the usual one adopted by bishops, priests, deacons, catechists, teachers, parents, and all who wish to hand on the faith. It is didactic (a teaching style) and magisterial. It can be adapted to the age and condition of the recipient, as is evident in the numerous books for children on this or that aspect of faith. Many a parish presentation in discussion groups and RCIA classes benefits from this approach. It is often found in pamphlets explaining this or that article of the creed or the *Catechism*. Most theologians switch to this style of theology when required to do so in order to explain doctrine, to catechize, evangelize, and defend aspects of Christianity. Examples abound: see, for instance, selected writings of Christoph Schönborn, Avery Dulles, Gerald O'Collins, Joseph Ratzinger, Hans Urs von Balthasar, Peter Kreeft, and William Most (d. 1999).

As a further note, it could be said that the theological work done in seminaries, religious communities, and houses of formation tends to be influenced by this style of theology. The intention is that future ministers receive a comprehensive presentation of and grounding in the Catholic faith: that they will be familiar with the main positions and arguments relating to the doctrines, sacraments, moral teaching, and canonical decrees they will have to implement and hand on through homilies, talks, presentations, and pastoral activity. Indeed, the doctrinal-catechetical style of theology leads naturally to pastoral studies, to canon law, and to the appropriate methods of the pastoral care of the faithful.

Some observations are in order. Stylistically speaking, this approach naturally looks more toward the past than the present—that is, toward a retrieval of the tradition and its sources in order to offer an exposition of true doctrine. It is therefore in general "conservative." It focuses on the primary sources of divine revelation—the Bible, tradition, and the statements of the church's magisterium—and less on the secondary sources of revelation and what can be known through creation, history, and personal experience. It tends to view revelation as essentially, albeit not exclusively, propositional, truths God has revealed for our enlightenment and for the right order of life both in the church and as disciples in the world. Its concern could be identified as truth and permanence, doctrine and piety, prayer and holiness.

As noted above, the doctrinal-catechetical style is theology as wisdom. It underlines the truth of revelation and invites believers to assent to that truth. It necessarily relies on a realistic philosophy, partly because of the facticity of the incarnation itself and partly because of the need to articulate with confidence truths that are definitive for human salvation. Consequently, its natural tendency is to draw on the classical inheritance of scholasticism and Aquinas. However, it could be argued that in this regard many practitioners unwittingly adopt a naive realism in their understanding of epistemology and the teachings of the church rather than a more nuanced or critical approach. In other words, the truths of faith tend to be perceived independently from the human experience, questions, insights, debate, reflection, and judgments that gave birth to them. This can lead to a quasi-fundamentalism or an unthinking type of faith.

Moreover, epistemologically the truth these doctrines contain tends to be perceived as "already-out-there-now-real," that is, as hard and solid facts, things anyone can see and that anyone ought therefore to believe and accept. The problem with this is that knowing is being understood as "taking a look"—I open my eyes and see the truth. From this point of view objectivity is a matter of seeing what is there to be seen, and reality is whatever is given in immediate sense experience. This naïve realism is an especially stubborn myth and a kind of default position on knowing for the Western mind, thanks to the fact that many of the words used for knowing in the Indo-European language group are related to seeing: e.g., the mind "sees" or "glimpses" a meaning; the truth "appears" or "comes into view." Many therefore think of knowing as essentially taking a look, opening the eyes and seeing, rather than as a complex cluster of ordered activities. They envisage the mind as a black box into which sense data flow and out of which speech comes. In any case, the real can never be simply a matter of receiving data presented by the senses. The real is what is intelligently grasped and reasonably affirmed. Otherwise belief in God—a spiritual Being—or belief in any reality that cannot be touched, tasted, seen, heard, and smelled—grace, for instance—would be untenable. Unfortunately, even many theologians think this way, without realizing that their philosophy is not as robust as they might like and in this case is actually undermining their belief.

The Critical-Historical Style

The second style of theology identified here is not the opposite of the first but its complement. This is academic theology. Whereas the first was concerned with doctrine, this style is concerned with systematics. The focus is not so much on the truth of doctrine—although the truth, with the arguments and context that prompted its historical evolution is indeed one of its concerns—but on its interpretation and meaning. Its aim is to interpret the Christian faith and to discuss and apply its meaning and value for life today. The context is often imagined by default, although not exclusively, to be the North Atlantic milieu, where faith and religion are in decline. There the critical-historical style of theology finds its natural home in the academy, in university faculties, and in theological journals and periodicals. It is the type of theology found in theology books, in the realm of biblical studies, in writings about church history, in academic departments and learned tomes, in conventions, seminars, lectures, and workshops called to consider old problems or new ideas, in the exchanges of scholars, in the commentaries of journalists, in the new studies of hermeneutics and critical methods, in the staff rooms of religious education departments. Theology done in this manner is connected with the dogmatic-catechetical style discussed before. It feeds into the thoughts and reflections of pastors and educators: the latest book on the priesthood, a new commentary on the Gospel of Mark, a revisionist history of Pius XII's proclamation of the dogma of the Assumption. Moreover, it derives its raison d'être from the church's doctrine, life, and worship. But it does all of this in a critical and quasi-independent fashion, examining how this or that definition of faith emerged, what difficulties people experience with current church teaching on sexual morality, exploring other possible ways of sharing power and authority within the church. This style of theology is not only at home with controversy and debate, it actually thrives on it. Its concern is less to defend, to judge, and to explain, and more to understand, to explore, to discuss reception, to marshal evidence, to hear new insights, to expose the past, and to open up new avenues for the future.

Go into the theology section of a large university or college library. On the one hand there will be collections of church documents, various philosophical, interreligious, and theological encyclopedias, volumes of church Fathers and selected reference works. There will be some books written in the doctrinal-catechetical style of theology mentioned above. There will also be some books in the contextual-experiential and transcendental styles to be discussed next. But the vast majority of the shelves will be filled with book after book typifying the critical-historical or academic approach under consideration here. Theology will be divided into various departments: biblical theology, patristics, the philosophy of religion, sacraments and liturgy, eschatology, moral theology, ecclesiology, Christology, fundamental theology, church history, and more. These will be subdivided into highly specialized sectors: the background to the Old Testament, the theologians of the Anglo-Catholic revival, the history of the church in Manchester, interreligious dialogue, theology of grace, tracts on hell and heaven, religious symbolism, and so on. Roman Catholic, Anglican, Methodist, Presbyterian, Orthodox: denominational labels are quite secondary as much of this style of theology is ecumenical, in many cases thoroughly so. A vast array of works on every possible topic related to religion and faith will be addressed by classical, recent, and contemporary theologians: Walter Kasper (b. 1933) on ecumenism, Thomas Groome on religious education, Hans Küng on infallibility, Carol Christ on feminist spirituality, William Abraham (b. 1947) on revelation, Edward Schillebeeckx on the sacraments, Thomas Reese (b. 1945) on the nature of episcopal conferences, Yves Congar on the Holy Spirit, Luke Timothy Johnson on the letter to the Hebrews, Henri de Lubac on medieval exegesis, Paul Knitter on theologies of religions, James Keenan on the commandments, Karl Rahner on the foundations of faith, Alcuin Reid on the liturgy, Thomas Rausch on ecclesiology, Paul Collins (b. 1940) on papal power, Thomas O'Meara (b. 1935) on ministry, Marcus Borg on the Synoptic account of the incarnation, Lisa Sowle Cahill on bioethics. Many of these theologians will belong to a particular school or stream of thought: Augustinian, Newmanian, Chestertonian, Rahnerian, Balthasarian, or whatever. The list of theologians, like the topics they address, is endless. Each is *sui generis*; each seeks to make her or his unique contribution and each adopts his or her own method, but what unites them all is that generally speaking, to a greater or lesser extent, they are all academic theologians.

This style of theology is termed "critical" in the sense that its focus is on critical understanding. This is theology in the long tradition of *fides quaerens intellectum*, a theology that identifies the difficulties, demonstrates the problems, points out the disagreements, and ventilates the grievances. It is also theology that accords with Lonergan's notion of a mediation between religion and its cultural matrix: it seeks to enter into critical conversation with the issues of the moment.

This style of theology is also termed "historical." In general it takes historical context and culture and the historical transmission of the Christian faith seriously. It can also be directly historical in its account. Subjects and topics might often be approached historically. But unlike in the previous style of theology, the purpose this time is to get behind the judgments and decisions of the past. By retrieving the basic questions that had arisen and the insights that were obtained it seeks to evaluate the processes by which later judgments were made. In other words, by its nature this style of theology will be more revisionist and progressivist than the previous style, more distant from the everyday belief of the faithful yet possibly more committed to changing the present and future than conserving the past, even though most theologians happily choose to swim within the broad river of the tradition. In the best theologians we see a withdrawal for the sake of a return, a critical reflection on faith for the sake of contributing to the daily life and advance of the church. This is why the tradition is often approached as a human social reality. An *epoché* of faith is made so that sources such as the Scriptures can be approached afresh and their meaning for today be revisited and interpreted. Of course, writers can be selective, even highly and deliberately so, in the material they discuss, but this is often picked up in later debate as other scholars point out the oversights that have occurred. The critical-historical style of theology evinces the self-corrective process of human learning as articles, periodicals, and books bring to light the deficiencies of previous scholarship.

Again, some observations are in order. First, this style of theology generally operates from below: it is not theology deduced from doctrines and fixed premises—although doctrines may be present implicitly or in the background like riverbanks channeling the river's flow—but rather theology that treats Scripture and tradition more in the manner of data to be investigated in the original context or in the light of contemporary techniques and procedures. Consequently it tends to view revelation less as propositions and more as a historical communication, a message with a meaning. Christ founded a community of disciples with teachings, structures, and practices that need to be investigated in order to ascertain their meaning. This is why the library shelves are full of the fruits of modern critical scholarship, the insights of Scripture scholars and church historians, philosophers of religion, and patristic experts. What was established and what does it mean? How can we rightly understand the Gospel and its meaning for us today? Moreover, while the primary sources of revelation are in view, theologians also explore the secondary sources and what can be known through creation, history, and personal experience in order to communicate the meaning and value of revelation to their audience. This gives this style of theology its more speculative emphasis.

Second, while, like the doctrinal-catechetical style, this critical-historical style is theology as wisdom, its focus is on understanding. It is theology seeking information, the new data uncovered leading to new insights and a more comprehensive viewpoint. Because of this focus on meaning, the critical-historical style of theology consciously or unconsciously adopts the classical, modern, and postmodern philosophies and philosophical commitments discussed in chapter 3. Yet this is where forms of philosophical idealism can sometimes enter in. In matters of faith, idealism can lead to an uncritical adoption of perspectives that view revelation through current thinking: that is, for those in the postmodern and plural-ist Western cultures, through modernist or relativist lenses.

Philosophically, like the naïve realism mentioned before, idealism causes the world to be perceived as "already-out-there-now-real," a world of "hard and solid" facts or things that anyone can see and that anyone ought to believe and accept. Knowing, in other words, is "taking a look." But this time, because of the Kantian dilemma, the looking is never conclusive because what can be seen are appearances and these may be perceptive. Consequently, we may have to settle for a theory or a hypo-thesis rather than a solid, once-and-for-all-time truth or conclusion. As before, the mind is envisaged as a black box into which sense data flow and out of which speech comes, but this time the sense data are always questionable and so we can never be sure of whatever comes out.

The result is that the "facts," in this case the truths of faith, can only be perceived as they appear within their historical sources. That they may be permanent truths of faith can be lost sight of. This can lead to multiple and endlessly conflicting interpretations that can only be judged on grounds of power or expediency, the triumph of one school or group over another, this authority or that theologian over the others. It all depends on perspective and on the one who manages to capture the popular media or the papal ear. This is why, for some, the permanent truth of doctrine is elusive; all that can exist are theological propositions to be contingently affirmed as the best result so far. In this conception the role of the magisterium is to police the traffic. Sometimes bad drivers may need to be cautioned, but the court is one in which the jury is always out and the judge's sentence ever contestable.

Contextual-Experiential Approaches

Here and there on the library shelves can also be found a small but growing number of theological works that evince another, quite distinc-tive style. This third style is the contextual and experiential approach. The turn to experience is something that has always been part of spir-ituality, writings on prayer, and advice on personal spiritual growth and development. This turn to experience within spirituality gathered pace through the twentieth century. Indeed, modern spiritual writings, it can be argued, now differ markedly in content, scope, and tone from what is depicted by, say, Adolphe Tanquerey (d. 1932) in his treatise *The Spiri-tual Life* (1923). To retrieve and transpose their content and teaching often requires considerable investment of time and reflection. But theology too, especially since the 1950s, has adopted a much more experiential and narrative tone both in terms of religious experience and conversion and in treating seriously the social, political, and historical context of believers. In the 1970s this was evident in the liberation and activist theologies of the time, but in the 1980s and 1990s new contextual theologies and theological tendencies came to the fore in missiology.

As the Nigerian-born Francis Oborji (*Concepts of Mission*, 2006) points out, contextual theologies both represent the experience and thought forms of Third World Christians and also seek to apply the Christian message to the sociocultural, political, and economic realities of their regions. They tend to be thoroughly ecumenical in approach and to take seriously the seeds of the Word in native religions. They emphasize Christology and inculturation in catechesis, liturgy, and interreligious dialogue and also, often with gusto, address issues relating to human liberation, social development, and justice. Many of the thinkers who write in this style belong to the Ecumenical Association of Third World Theologians (EATWOT), begun in Tanzania in 1976. They might be roughly grouped into three categories: (1) those from Latin America, such as Gustavo Gutiérrez and the liberation theologians mentioned in chapter 2; (2) those from Asia: the Indian theologians Durasaimy S. Amalorpavadass (d. 1990), Raimon Panikkar (b. 1918), and Michael Amaladoss (b. 1936), often concerned with "cosmic Christology," the Korean people's ("Minjung") theology, and Japanese theologians such as Kazoh Kitamori (b. 1916) and Kosuke Koyama (b. 1929), whose writings have been much concerned with the dialogue with Buddhism; and (3) those from the rich diversity of Africa, such as the Congolese priest Benezet Bujo, who writes on ancestral religion. Nearly all these theologies are critical equally of North Atlantic theology and of Western socioeconomic exploitation. Their critiques have in turn helped Western theology to become much more conscious of its own limitations and its universalist and normative pretensions.

Indeed, as missionary theologians such as Stephen Bevans (b. 1944), Roger Schroeder (b. 1951), and Robert Schreiter, who write on global currents in missiology, point out, Western theologians themselves have become increasingly aware of their own contextual issues. This had already been occurring in, for instance, feminist, womanist, gay-lesbian, and environmentalist theologies. But more than that, the argument is that Western theologians need to take their general context much more seriously if they are to allow the contextual theologies from the world's South to enjoy an equal footing within the church. For just as the Christian church has been much enriched from its historic inculturation in Greco-Roman Western forms, so now, it is argued, its passage through the cultures of Asia, Africa, and the world's South needs to be permitted to make a lasting contribution to the universal church's common heritage.

These localized theologies are in the critical-historical style of theology, but with a crucial difference. Instead of being focused on the object of faith, they attend closely to the subject, the recipient of faith, and the meaning of the Gospel for his or her local culture. This is theology with a preferential option for the local subject. It claims to take real account of the qualities, conditions, and cultural background: black, white, poor, rich, language, nationality, man, woman, minority or majority, the religious background, and so on. Consequently, this is not theology in the wisdom tradition. This is theology, like liberation theology, that seeks social transformation, change, and integral human development: *fides quaerens actionem*. Indeed, many of the contextual theologians reject what they see as Western-style academic theology as irrelevant to praxis, or at least to the kind of praxis needed in their context.

As with the previous style, this is again theology done from below, a theology done *in situ*. It requires an in-depth knowledge of the history, customs, and religions of a society, and a judgment about possible socioeconomic and political options. It is interdisciplinary. Its style and tone are highly evaluative and exhortatory, calling to action for justice. It tends to be at least as much focused on concrete circumstances as on matters internal to the church. As with liberation theologies, it often finds its starting point in the historical Jesus and the proclamation of the kingdom. It has an eschatological direction that looks forward to the New Earth.

Two observations: First, theologies that adopt a contextual-experiential style often regard revelation not as propositional truths or as historical meaning but as a prophetic word that challenges the status quo and goads humans into action. The goal of revelation is transforming action. It is a word being spoken in the here and now, and so the secondary sources of revelation become at least as crucial as the primary sources, sometimes more important than these for discerning God's will for us at this moment. The events of the Bible show a God at work on the side of the poor against the worldly rich and powerful. This is a paradigm for Christians today. To do God's work, the true disciple must join him and work for human transformation in a more just world. This is what the kingdom means. Truth is an important concern, but action is more important. Indeed, actions speak louder than words. Doctrines therefore are relative to their function as moral exhortations and blueprints for action. The older theologies with their concerns for metaphysics and ontology are potentially redundant ("Western" and "bourgeois") unless they can inform about right relationships and how to establish them.

Second, a philosophical difficulty can sometimes arise in this style of theology, namely, subjectivism and the question of the extent to which theologians might aspire to making anything more than subjective or contingent, historically conditioned judgments. The issue is again that of idealism and the underlying philosophical commitments contextual theologians make. The claim to speak definitively about a situation is itself a truth claim, but one that might be logically unsustainable where post-Kantian social and political philosophies have been adopted. In matters of faith, idealism can lead to an uncritical adoption of contextual and experiential viewpoints that regard revelation through philosophies of praxis in activist and political categories. This can be both enriching and limiting. The claim to speak from a particular personal, historical, or cultural experience is arguably an enrichment of theology, but the realm of experience also needs to be enlarged to take in the experience of others, including those of our Christian forebears and of other Christians, even those of the North Atlantic region. Otherwise theology runs the danger of relativism or a factionalism that privileges one group over another.

An authentically Catholic approach incorporates tradition as well as Scripture. To treat tradition as historically contingent and its Greco-Roman, medieval, and Western inculturation as distortions or unnecessary baggage or as largely irrelevant to the needs of the world's South is difficult to reconcile with *Dei Verbum*. It results in a campaign for wholesale deconstruction and reconstruction in order to purge and purify the local church from Western accretions. Instead, what might arguably be more authentic and of greater benefit would be an integral if frank exchange within a communion of churches committed to pursuing a just outcome.

The Transcendental Approach

Finally, the transcendental approach is a distinctive style within academic theology practiced by a small but growing number of theologians. It is typified by the thought of Karl Rahner and those influenced by him such as Leo O'Donovan (b. 1934), Herbert Vorgrimler, Heinrich Fries, Heinz Schlette, and a number of Protestant and Reformed theologians, including John Macquarrie (d. 2007) and George Lindbeck. Rahner's achievement was discussed above. It is noted here under the label "transcendental" because of its distinctive claim to have retrieved the thought of Aquinas in the light of the epistemological and the existential concerns of Kant and Heidegger. Rahner claims to have shown how God is intended in every human act of knowing, freedom, and love. This gives his writing a distinctive character in which God is portrayed as the mysterious and ever-receding horizon of the human spirit.

A similar trajectory operates in the thought of Bernard Lonergan and those writers influenced by the philosophy, theology, and methodology of *Insight: A Study of Human Understanding* (1957) and *Method in Theology* (1972). This will form an extended focus here, in part because Lonergan's achievement attracts universal acclaim even if its adoption in practice remains embryonic. Indeed, his method outshines all other contemporary efforts at devising a serviceable approach for the new postconciliar situation within theology, and he has clarified some of the most complex and radical philosophical and methodological issues theology currently faces. The key challenge is the initial effort required to master it. Even so, a growing number of Lonerganian scholars have taken up the challenge, including Frederick Crowe (b. 1915), a veritable polymath Lonerganian scholar; Frederick Lawrence (b. 1944) and Matthew Lamb (b. 1933), who have written on social and political philosophy; Charles Hefling (b. 1949) of Boston College; Philip McShane (b. 1932), an editor of Lonergan's works on economics; the Scripture scholar Ben Meyer, a key influence on N. T. Wright; and Tad Dunne (b. 1938), author of several books on spirituality.

Lonergan sought to rewrite the method for Catholic philosophy and theology so that it could enter into a critical conversation with modern science and scholarship. He wanted to provide solid foundations, a secure base so that theologians might authentically retrieve the tradition and yet be able to engage confidently with the new *quaestiones disputatae* raised by modern scholarship, and also to establish a critical dialogue with the human sciences. In fact, the method he proposed was arguably continuous with the classical heritage of Augustine and Aquinas and yet at the same time enhanced that tradition along new lines with a new foundation. It can be viewed in a number of ways: as a process for doing theology, as a means or mechanism to foster collaboration between theologians, and as an approach that enables theology to become more relational and interdisciplinary.

Lonergan began from an analysis of human consciousness: the head, the will, and the heart. *Insight* was chiefly about how understanding and knowing works. Lonergan claimed to discover an invariant pattern or structure of interrelated activities operative in knowing. He characterized these by the three general terms "experiencing," "understanding," and "judging." In *Method* he explored the moral and religious dimensions of human decision making, action, and love, applying his "understanding of understanding" to religion, culture, and the Christian faith. He sought to retrieve and identify the various activities associated with "deciding," and he named this as a fourth level after the first three levels of experiencing, understanding, and judging.

Lonergan's argument is that all human knowing, choosing, and loving are normatively patterned and so the interrelated cognitional and volitional operations of the human mind itself can act as a meta-method by which knowing, doing, and loving can operate in each particular field. In other words, he conceived the basic transcendental pattern of operations as a structure that could function in every particular discipline, including theology:

> Transcendental method offers a key to unified science. . . . [For] in harmony with all development is the human mind itself, which effects the developments. In unity with all fields, however disparate, is . . . the human mind that operates in all fields and in radically the same fashion in each. Through the self-knowledge, the self-appropriation, the self-possession that result from making explicit the basic normative pattern of the recurrent and related operations of human cognitional process, it becomes possible to envisage a future in which all workers in all fields can find in transcendental method common norms, foundations, systematics, and common critical, dialectical and heuristic procedures. (Bernard Lonergan, *Method in Theology*, 24)

As in a computer the operating system enables all sorts of different applications to run on it, so, according to Lonergan, the innate structures and operations of the human person lend to all knowing and choosing a fundamental and essential unity.

In the 1960s Lonergan claimed a further breakthrough that enabled him to modulate the method specifically to theology, namely, "functional specialization." His new insight was the realization that theology, like many historical and scholarly endeavors, operates in two phases: reception and transmission. In other words, theologians have to investigate the past and go back to the sources in order to apply their meaning to the issues of the present. To teach, explain, and communicate something means first to research, understand, and grasp it. Consequently Lonergan envisaged theology as comprising two phases (see figure 15). The first involves listening to God's Word: researching the sources and the tradition in order to appropriate their data, meanings, history, and basic positions. The

second phase involves bearing witness to God's Word: communicating to
the present what has been discovered, applying its spirit, teaching, meaning, and message to the world of today. Since there are four levels of
cognitional and volitional operations, there are eight functional specialties,
four to retrieve the past and four to express the tradition for the present.

LONERGAN'S METHOD FOR THEOLOGY		
PHASE ONE RETRIEVING THE TRADITION "LISTENING TO THE WORD"		**PHASE TWO** ENGAGING WITH CULTURE "BEARING WITNESS TO WORD"
FS 4 DIALECTICS (witness) • Evaluating what has emerged from FS 1-3, reaching a critical, comprehensive viewpoint about the conflicts of history, eliminating false starts (e.g., is there real conflict between Vatican I and Vatican II?) • Leads to articles, books, lectures	DECIDING basic positions	FS 5 FOUNDATIONS (faith) • Where do I stand? Where does my community stand? Stating how I or my community confronts the past and saying what is true theologically and spiritually • Leads to conversion, articles, books, lectures
FS 3 HISTORY (context) • Constructing a history of the time, saying what was happening, contextualizing movements • Leads to chronicles, articles, books	JUDGING facts and beliefs	FS 6 DOCTRINES (beliefs) • Affirming what one has discovered and the community holds dear, affirming judgments, teaching, dogma • Leads to statements (e.g., magisterium)
FS 2 INTERPRETATION (meaning) • Discovering the meaning of the data or coming to understand it: cf. work of biblical exegesis, hermeneutics • Often leads to commentaries	UNDERSTANDING meanings (past/present)	FS 7 SYSTEMATICS (explanation) • Explaining, relating, and inter-relating Christian foundations and doctrines with the cultural context • Leads to books, articles, guides, etc.
FS 1 RESEARCH (data) • Gathering artifacts, texts, data: e.g., work of archaeology, textual criticism, study of sources • Often leads to encyclopedias, dictionaries	EXPERIENCING/ COMMUNICATING the data	FS 8 COMMUNICATIONS (pastoral) • Passing on the message through preaching, catechesis, media (art, writing, music, film, etc.) • Leads to pastoral theology, studies, skills, etc.

Figure 15

As a way of doing theology, each functional specialty (here FS) is meant
to produce outcomes appropriate to the level of operation to which it is

related, although every theologian in every specialty operates on all four levels. The outcome of those who do research (FS 1)—that is, the fruit of their dispassionate experience, penetrating intelligence, wise judgment, and prudent choice—is the exact data. Those who specialize in interpretation and exegesis (FS 2) describe the real meaning. The historians (FS 3) present what actually happened. Dialecticians (FS 4) evaluate history and its disputes, indicating the real winners and losers. Foundational theologians (FS 5) explain and defend their convictions and those of the ecclesial community. Dogmatic theologians (FS 6) establish the church's teaching. Systematic theologians (FS 7) expound the meaning of the church's doctrines for the modern world and its questions, while pastoral theologians (FS 8) specialize in expressing the message in appropriate language and formats for its many and diverse addressees.

However, Lonergan's method for theology was not a static division into subject areas; it was, rather, a mechanism to channel the flow. A possible analogy would be to think of a hospital in which each specialist is working for the general goal of healing the sick while specializing in the activities appropriate to her or his specialization. Thus the ancillary workers are as important as the doctors, the ambulance crews as critical as the surgeons, the work of the laboratories as important as the work of the kitchen. The aim is to process the patient from being received into the accident and emergency department through the many intermediate stages of diagnosis, treatment, surgery, and rehabilitation to his or her return to home and work, fully recovered.

In Lonergan's proposal, each FS is critical to the outcome of the whole and each, while autonomous, is nonetheless functionally related to every other FS. None can be omitted or deemed more important than another. Biblical studies (FS 1 and FS 2) do not control systematic theology (FS 7), yet they do remotely and sometimes directly establish some of its terms and conditions. Specialties are successive; one follows the other, and each adds something to the next. Systematic theology (FS 7) follows from dogmatic (FS 6), while providing pastoral theology (FS 8) with its project, yet without ignoring the results of prior disciplines such as biblical scholarship (FS 1 and FS 2) and history (FS 3 and FS 4). Lonergan's proposal therefore seeks to clarify the overall process of theology from gathering data to achieving results, sharing the various tasks to be done.

As a way of coordinating theologians, Lonergan's proposal envisages theology as fundamentally collaborative. The principal responsibilities of the magisterium (FS 6), theologians (FS 7), and pastors (FS 8) are laid forth in terms of judgments (doctrine), understanding (explanations), and experience (communication). The method gives specialists a map, a vision of the totality and location of their specialization. The biblical scholar, the historian, the fundamental theologian, the systematician, and the pastor need to keep an eye on each other. At present specialists in one field tend to find it difficult to communicate with those in others. Totalitarianisms are often at work. Again, where one specialty is absent others often rush in to fill the gap, even though the new disciplines lack the detailed knowledge and methods that belong to the missing discipline.

Finally, the proposed method is designed to make theology a fundamentally interdisciplinary activity. Lonergan envisaged theology as engaged in dialogue with other areas of knowing, especially modern science and scholarship. He defines the task of theology, as was noted before in chapter 1, as a mediation "between a cultural matrix and the significance and role of a religion in that matrix." In other words, the task of theologians is to investigate the sources of religion in order to communicate its meaning to contemporary culture. They also have to listen to the questions and issues being raised by contemporary culture in order to put them to the sources of their religion. In this way theology becomes the means by which religion and culture enter into a critical conversation:

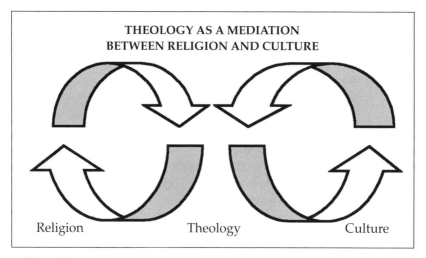

**THEOLOGY AS A MEDIATION
BETWEEN RELIGION AND CULTURE**

Religion   Theology   Culture

Figure 16

Lonergan's proposal raises in itself many complex questions. It has met with mixed reactions. Did he propose that eventually every theology faculty would have eight departments? Did he envisage every theology faculty eventually renaming and reordering the scope and work of its theologians to fit the nomenclature and parameters suggested by functional specialization? Did he suppose that every theology book or paper would eventually treat this or that topic in eight chapters or sections? *Method in Theology* certainly seems to invite theologians and theology departments to move in those directions, even if the proposal is one for the long term. The unfamiliar terminology, the very general and difficult nature of the terrain, the personal investment required in self-appropriation, the philosophical commitment needed, the welter of questions and issues raised, the dearth of adequate secondary literature, the paucity of successful examples of the method in practice, and even the lingering issue of its relevance or immediacy to the particular theological task at hand have put many off. To grasp the method for oneself in its depth and richness is a major achievement, and such a personal commitment would need to be replicated among colleagues if the full benefits were to be realized in an ongoing collaboration.

On the other hand, we might add two more positive observations about this transcendental style of theology, and in particular the proposed method of Bernard Lonergan. First, theologians who adopt Lonergan's approach would seem to benefit from Lonergan's fuller anthropology of the human person as intellectual, volitional, and cordial, and as both personal and social. As a consequence, at least in theory, this style of theology could take into account the characteristics of all the other styles mentioned before: the sapiential, the moral-activist, and the spiritual. Moreover, since Lonergan gives extensive consideration to the Inner Word of God's love operative in human hearts, his implicit understanding of revelation might be richer than that often found in other styles of theology: revelation can still be propositional, in the sense of truths of faith to be believed, but also historical as meanings given in history, and not least as spiritual, the fruit of grace and the inner workings of the Holy Spirit. As with the doctrinal-catechetical and critical-historical styles of theologizing, Lonergan's method emphasizes the retrieval of the tradition, but not necessarily in a positivistic or modernistic manner. The intention is a critical differentiation of the true and lasting core from the historically conditioned penumbra. On the other hand, since the intended purpose of the method is to communicate with the present, it could be argued that Lonergan's method also meets the needs and realities identified by the contextual-experiential styles of theology, though again only in terms of an authentic and critical engagement. It requires theologians to understand in depth the culture to which the Gospel message is to be communicated and the transformations it should bring about.

Second, this style of theology does make the turn to the subject, but this need not imply a subjectivism or, for that matter, an epistemological idealism that seeks to distort doctrine or reduces it to theological opinion. Lonergan espouses a critical realism: that is, one that does not envisage knowing as "taking a look" but sees it as a compound of different activities. Truth is not the already-out-there-now-real, but that which is intelligently grasped in understanding and reasonably affirmed in judgment. In judgment, according to Lonergan, the mind grasps the truth from the convergence of possibilities, after having worked out the conditions of possibility, grasped whether those conditions have been fulfilled, and made the judgment that no further questions are required. In this schema objectivity is the fruit of authentic subjectivity: that is, true judgments result from the authentically operating subject.

Perhaps some of the objections to Lonergan's method have already been or could easily be addressed. Even so, it still behooves Lonerganian scholars to communicate Lonergan's thought more effectively if there is to be, as many would hope, a second reception and a more widespread diffusion of his ideas. Indeed, it could be argued that when Lonergan was writing, in the late 1960s and early 1970s, consideration of theological method was an interesting but hardly a frontline activity. Today, however, in the early twenty-first century, the rampant pluralism and vibrant development of Catholic theology makes thought about method no longer a luxury but a necessity if the unity of faith and the multiple gains made in recent decades, especially since the Vatican Council, are to be consolidated and not lost.

Appendix

Excerpts from the
First Vatican General Council
(Third Session):
Dei Filius (Dogmatic Constitution
on the Catholic Faith, 1870)[1]

1. From the Introduction:

To meet the numerous problems of the time, Pope Pius IX summoned the 20th General Council. It met in the Vatican from December 1869 to September 1870. From the many drafts proposed to the Council only two constitutions were finalized, the first on the catholic faith, the second on the primacy and infallibility of the Pope (cf. n. 813ff.). In the four chapters of the Constitution on the Catholic Faith and in the corresponding canons, the Church set forth its doctrine against the current errors of the 19th century: materialism, rationalism, pantheism, and also against the inner-catholic approaches of fideism and traditionalism. The first chapter deals with God and creation (cf. n. 412-413); the second with revelation, its relation to human reason, and the channels of Scripture and Tradition through which revelation is communicated; the third chapter treats of faith, its rational and supernatural foundations and its place in the Christian life;

---

[1] The selections here are from chapter 2, "Revelation," and chapter 4, "Faith and Reason." The introduction and the translation of the text are from Jacques Dupuis, ed., *The Christian Faith in the Doctrinal Documents of the Catholic Church*, 7th revised and enlarged edition (New York: Alba House, 2001).

the fourth enters into the complex problems of the relation between faith and reason.

The doctrine of the council is expressed in terms of 19th-century theology. Revelation is presented primarily as the communication of supernatural truth inaccessible to natural reason, and faith as the submissive acceptance of this revealed truth. The Second Vatican Council will later complement this doctrine with a more personalist approach, according to which God speaks to human beings as to friends, whom he invites to communion of life with himself, through Christ, in the Holy Spirit. Faith then freely accepts this invitation in a commitment of one's whole self.[2]

2. From Chapter Two: Revelation

(Natural knowledge of God and supernatural revelation)[3]

The same Holy Mother Church holds and teaches that God, the source and end of all things, can be known with certainty from the things that were created, through the natural light of human reason, for "ever since the creation of the world his invisible nature has been clearly perceived in the things that have been made" [Rom 1:20]; but that it pleased his wisdom and bounty to reveal himself and his eternal decrees in another, supernatural way, as the apostle says: "In many and various ways God spoke of old to our fathers by the prophets; but in these last days he has spoken to us by a Son" [Heb 1:1-21].

(The necessity of divine revelation)[4]

It is to be ascribed to this divine revelation that such truths about things divine which of themselves are not beyond human reason can, even in the present condition of humankind, be known by everyone with facility, with firm certitude and with no admixture of error. It is, however, not for this reason that revelation is to be judged absolutely necessary, but because God in His infinite goodness has ordained us to a supernatural end, viz., to share in the good things of God which utterly exceed the intelligence of the human mind, for "no eye has seen, nor ear heard, nor the human heart conceived, what God prepared for those who love him" [1 Cor 2:9].

[2] *The Christian Faith*, 42–43.
[3] ND 113/DS 3004.
[4] ND 114/DS 3005.

3. From Chapter Four: Faith And Reason

(The twofold order of religious knowledge)[5]

The perpetual common belief of the Catholic Church has held and holds also this: there is a twofold order of knowledge, distinct not only in its source but also in its object; in its source, because in the one we know by natural reason, in the other by divine faith; in its object, because apart from what natural reason can attain, there are proposed to our belief mysteries that are hidden in God, which can never be known unless they are revealed by God. Hence the apostle who, on the one hand, testifies that God is known to the gentiles by means of the things that have been made [cf. Rom 1:20-21], on the other hand, when speaking about the grace and truth that came through Jesus Christ [cf. John 1:17], proclaims: "We speak the wisdom of God in a mystery, a wisdom which is hidden, which God ordained before the world unto our glory, which none of the princes of this world knew. . . . But to us God has revealed this by his Spirit. For the Spirit searches everything, even the deep things of God" [1 Cor 2:7-10 Vulg.]. The only begotten himself praises the Father because he has hidden these things from the wise and understanding and has revealed them to little ones [cf. Mt 11:25].

(Task and limits of reason)[6]

Nevertheless, if reason illumined by faith inquires in an earnest, pious and sober manner, it attains by God's grace a certain understanding of the mysteries, which is most fruitful, both from the analogy with the objects of its natural knowledge and from the connection of these mysteries with one another and with our ultimate end. But it never becomes capable of understanding them in the way it does the truths which constitute its proper object. For divine mysteries by their very nature so excel the created intellect that even when they have been communicated in revelation and received by faith, they remain covered by the veil of faith itself and shrouded as it were in darkness as long as in this mortal life "we are away from the Lord, for we walk by faith, not by sight" (2 Cor 5:6-7).

---

[5] ND 131/DS 3015.
[6] ND 132/DS 3016.

(Faith and reason cannot contradict each other)[7]

However, though faith is above reason, there can never be a real conflict between faith and reason, since the same God who reveals mysteries and infuses faith has bestowed the light of reason on the human mind, and God cannot deny himself, nor can truth ever contradict truth. The deceptive appearance of such a contradiction is mainly due to the fact that either the dogmas of faith have not been understood and expounded according to the mind of the church, or that uncertain theories are taken for verdicts of reason. Thus "we define that every assertion that is opposed to enlightened faith is utterly false" (Lateran V: DS 1441).

Further,[8] the Church which, along with the apostolic office of teaching, received the charge of guarding the deposit of faith has also from God the right and the duty to proscribe what is falsely called knowledge (cf. 1 Tim 6:20), lest anyone be deceived by philosophy and vain fallacy (cf. Col 2:8). Hence all believing Christians are not only forbidden to defend as legitimate conclusions of science such opinions which they realize to be contrary to the doctrine of faith, particularly if they have been condemned by the Church, but they are seriously bound to account them as errors which put on the fallacious appearance of truth.

(Mutual support of faith and reason)[9]

Not only can there be no conflict between faith and reason, but they also support each other since right reason demonstrates the foundations of faith and, illumined by its light, pursues the understanding of divine things, while faith frees and protects reason from errors and provides it with manifold insights. It is therefore far removed from the truth to say that the Church opposes the study of human arts and sciences; on the contrary, she supports and promotes them in many ways. She does not ignore or despise the benefits that human life derives from them. Indeed, she confesses: as they have their origin from God who is the Lord of knowledge (cf. 1 Sam 2:3), so too, if rightly pursued, they lead to God with the help of his grace. Nor does the Church in any way forbid that these sciences, each in its sphere, should make use of their own principles and of the method proper to them. While, however, acknowledging this just freedom, she seriously warns lest they fall into error by going contrary to divine doctrine, or, stepping beyond their own limits, they enter into the sphere of faith and create confusion.

---

[7] ND 133/DS 3017.
[8] ND 134/DS 3018.
[9] ND 135/DS 3019.

4. Canons on Chapter IV [10]

1. If anyone says that in divine revelation no true and properly so called mysteries are contained but that all dogmas of faith can be understood and demonstrated from natural principles by reason, if it is properly trained, *anathema sit*.

2. If anyone says that human sciences are to be pursued with such liberty that their assertions, even if opposed to revealed doctrine, may he held as true and cannot be proscribed by the Church, *anathema sit*.

3. If anyone says that, as science progresses, at times a sense is to be given to dogmas proposed by the Church, different from the one which the Church has understood and understands, *anathema sit*.

---

[10] ND 137/DS 3041; ND 138/DS 3042; ND 139/DS 3043.

Bibliography

Audi, Robert, ed. *The Cambridge Dictionary of Philosophy*. 2nd ed. Cambridge: Cambridge University Press, 1999.

Carey, Patrick W., and Joseph T. Lienhard, eds. *Biographical Dictionary of Christian Theologians*. Peabody, MA: Hendrickson, 2002.

Dulles, Avery Cardinal, SJ. *Magisterium: Teacher and Guardian of the Faith*. Naples, FL: Sapientia Press of Ave Maria University, 2007.

Dupuis, Jacques, ed. *The Christian Faith in the Doctrinal Documents of the Catholic Church*. 7th rev. and enlarged ed. New York: Alba House, 2001.

Kerr, Fergus. *Twentieth-Century Catholic Theologians: From Neoscholasticism to Nuptial Mysticism*. Oxford: Blackwell, 2007.

Lonergan, Bernard, SJ. "Dimensions of Meaning." In *Collected Works of Bernard Lonergan*, vol. 4. Edited by Frederick E. Crowe and Robert M. Doran. Toronto: University of Toronto Press, 1988.

———. *Method in Theology*. London: Darton, Longman and Todd, 1972.

———. *Philosophical and Theological Papers 1965–1980. Collected Works of Bernard Lonergan*, vol. 17. Edited by Robert C. Croken and Robert M. Doran. Toronto: University of Toronto Press, 2004.

———. "Theology and Man's Future." In *Papers by Bernard J. F. Lonergan, S.J.* Edited by William F. J. Ryan and Bernard J. Tyrrell. London: Darton, Longman and Todd, 1974.

McBrien, Richard P., ed. *The HarperCollins Encyclopedia of Catholicism*. New York: HarperCollins, 1995.

Newman, John Henry. *An Essay on the Development of Christian Doctrine*. London: Longman, Green and Co., 3rd edition, 1878.

O'Collins, Gerald and Edward G. Farrugia, eds. *A Concise Dictionary of Theology*. Rev. and expanded ed. Mahwah, NJ: Paulist Press, 2000.

Ott, Ludwig. *Fundamentals of Catholic Dogma*. Edited by James Canon Bastible. Translated by Patrick Lynch. Rockford, IL: TAN Books and Publishers, 1974.

Rowland, Tracey. *Culture and the Thomist Tradition: After Vatican II*. London: Routledge, 2003.

Schwarz, Hans. *Theology in a Global Context: The Last Two Hundred Years*. Grand Rapids, MI: Eerdmans, 2005.

Index